Basic Facts About
Assessment of
DYSLEXIA
Testing for Teaching

Basic Facts About
Assessment of
DYSLEXIA
Testing for Teaching

by Susan C. Lowell, M.A., B.C.E.T.,
Rebecca H. Felton, Ph.D.,
& Pamela Hook, Ph.D.

The International Dyslexia Association, Inc.
Baltimore, Maryland

The
International
DYSLEXIA
Association®

Promoting literacy through research, education, and advocacy.™
Founded in Memory of Dr. Samuel T. Orton

The membership of the International Dyslexia Association (IDA) promotes understanding and support of individuals with dyslexia and other learning problems. The headquarters office in Baltimore, Maryland provides information and referral services to thousands of people every year. *The IDA Knowledge and Practice Standards* outline what all teachers of reading should know and be able to do to teach reading in regular education, preventive, intervention, or remedial settings. These standards are the metric for IDA's accreditation of preparation programs and certification of individuals. IDA accreditation and certification ensure that all students, especially those with dyslexia, will receive the structured literacy instruction that they need to learn to read well and reach their potential.

For more information on IDA and membership, accreditation, and certification contact

The International Dyslexia Association
40 York Road, 4th Floor
Baltimore, MD 21204-5202
Telephone: (410) 296-0232
(800) ABC-D123
Fax: (410) 321-5069
www.eida.org

Composition by Mid-Atlantic Design and Print, Inc.
Cover Illustration by Julia Hansen/123RF Stock Photo
Printed in the United States of America by Lightning Source.

Publisher's Cataloging-In-Publication Data
(Prepared by The Donohue Group, Inc.)

Lowell, Susan C., 1955-
    Basic facts about assessment of dyslexia : testing for teaching / by Susan C. Lowell, M.A., B.C.E.T., Rebecca H. Felton, Ph.D., & Pamela Hook, Ph.D.
    pages : illustration ; cm. — (Basic facts series ; [book 2])
    Includes bibliographical references.
    ISBN: 978-0-89214-068-8
    1. Dyslexia. 2. Reading—Ability testing. 3. Reading—Remedial teaching. 4. Dyslexic children—Education. 5. Educational tests and measurements. I. Felton, Rebecca Hobgood. II. Hook, Pamela E. III. Title.
LB1050.5 .L69 2014
371.9144   2014950297

For Duston, who always knew, and for Dr. Isabelle Y. Liberman.
Susan C. Lowell, M.A., B.C.E.T.

For all of the students and parents who have taught us
many lessons about life and reading.
Rebecca H. Felton, Ph.D.

For Dr. Doris Johnson, my mentor, to whom I owe so much.
Pamela Hook, Ph.D.

"Once you learn to read,
you will be forever free."
Frederick Douglas

Contents

About the Authors

Susan C. Lowell, M.A., B.C.E.T., a Fulbright Scholar, directs Educational Therapy Associates, a private clinical practice in Chapel Hill, North Carolina, and provides educational evaluations, consultations, advocacy, and teacher training. Ms. Lowell, a Board Certified Educational Therapist, specializes in diagnosis and remediation of learning difficulties including dyslexia. Ms. Lowell served as a vice president of the Board of Directors of the International Dyslexia Association (IDA) and is a past president of the North Carolina Branch of IDA. She is an Associate to the Advisory Committee on Exceptional Children of the Office of Overseas Schools, U.S. Department of State, and teaches a reading course for Buffalo State S.U.N.Y. in the graduate program. Ms. Lowell presents seminars and lectures on research-based components of reading instruction and assessment of reading difficulties internationally and in the United States. She is an adjunct faculty member at Simmons College in the IDA accredited graduate program, *Language and Literacy.*

Rebecca H. Felton, M.Ed., Ph.D., is currently in private practice in Southport, North Carolina, where she specializes in the assessment, diagnosis, and development of treatment plans for students with dyslexia. Dr. Felton taught students with disabilities for several years before beginning a career as a clinician and researcher with the Neurology Department of the Wake Forest University School of Medicine where she was a Co-Investigator of the National Institute of Child Health and Human Development (NICHD) supported studies of dyslexia. Teacher training has been a major focus of Dr.

Felton's career and, as a consultant to the North Carolina Department of Public Instruction, she developed a course on the foundations of reading, which has been used to train teachers throughout North Carolina for a number of years. As an adjunct professor, she developed and taught a course on the assessment of reading disabilities in the Simmons College *Language and Literacy* program, an IDA accredited graduate program. Dr. Felton is the author of a number of articles related to research in the area of dyslexia with a focus on early identification of students at risk, reading fluency, and interventions for students with severe reading problems.

Pamela Hook, Ph.D., taught for 20 years in the CSD Department at the MGH Institute of Health Professions where she is currently a Clinical Professor Emerita, having retired in 2012. She received her master's degree in reading from Harvard and her doctorate from the Communication Disorders/Learning Disabilities program at Northwestern. Dr. Hook has presented and written extensively on the topic of spoken and written language relationships. For over 30 years she has also consulted at Lexia Learning Systems, where she designed software, lessons, and paper-based materials to teach children and adults to read. Dr. Hook presently works as a Senior Scientist at Lexia in the areas of research and educational content design to create a blended curriculum for teaching reading and writing to typically developing and struggling readers.

Acknowledgments

The authors would like to thank the IDA Board of Directors and the IDA community for their support of this project. In particular, we would like to thank the members of the IDA Publications Committee, especially Louisa Moats and Karen Dakin, for their ongoing promotion of IDA publications. We are also very grateful to the wonderful Denise Douce at IDA for her editorial expertise.

Preface

Why is assessment of dyslexia important? Students and adults who come to schools or clinics for assessment of learning and literacy problems usually think they are not smart. Indeed, many students tell their parents, "I am so dumb," in frustration, sadness, and sometimes anger when they are not able to read and spell as easily as others in their classes.

Once students or adults know that they have a specific language-based learning disability called *dyslexia*, they understand that they are smart but that learning to read, spell, and write is difficult for them. They also appreciate why literacy is challenging because they recognize that the difficulties they face are language-based; their learning problems are not due to low intelligence or lack of motivation.

A diagnosis of dyslexia also helps the student, family, and educators formulate a plan to address the learning problems. They can access the large body of research about this prevalent learning disorder and learn about effective treatment and accommodations. They will feel secure knowing what works, utilizing information about research-based approaches and avoiding the controversial therapies not supported by research that can waste precious time and family resources.

After consultation about their diagnosis and recommendations for remediation and accommodations, students with dyslexia understand that the most effective treatment is instruction. Students with dyslexia need instruction from a highly skilled and well-trained reading teacher who has expertise about the structure of the language and who uses a research-based curriculum taught well, with fidelity.

Students with dyslexia need to spend more time than average on task learning to read, spell, and write. They also need accommodations for their learning problems that persist over the lifespan. Clinical reports with diagnostic statements can be used to provide access to specially designed instruction in schools and to provide needed accommodations in schools, universities, and the workplace as mandated by federal and state laws.

Finally, with appropriate diagnosis, individuals with dyslexia will better understand their own strengths and weaknesses and know how their assessment specifies the need for remediation and accommodations. They will feel secure, knowing they are in good company with the millions of bright and talented individuals who have this most common language-based learning disability and yet go on to have successful and rewarding personal and professional lives.

Because assessing dyslexia is so important to the success of so many, the authors have written this book to address the critical issues surrounding the diagnosis of this most common learning disability.

1
BECOMING A READER

Learning to read is the most important achievement for students in early education. Educators and parents agree that attaining literacy is vitally important for all students. When considering assessment for individuals who struggle with reading, spelling, and writing, it is helpful to consider the many factors that go into reading acquisition. Once students learn to read, they can begin to read to learn, and then the world of information and ideas becomes available to them.

Reading is a fairly new phenomenon in the history of human development, invented only a few thousand years ago. The human brain is actually wired for speech, and young children learn to speak naturally by experiencing language around them. Reading is not natural to humans; it takes direct and explicit instruction to master reading, spelling, and writing skills, and many students struggle or fail to achieve full literacy. Although some students learn to read and write with relative ease, all students need several years of instruction to progress from early readers, able to decode and spell simple words, to proficient readers, capable of reading, spelling, and writing with accuracy, automaticity, and ease. Accurate and fluent readers with well-developed vocabularies and knowledge of sentence structures typically have strong comprehension or understanding of the material they are reading. The development of good reading comprehension is vitally important and remains the main focus and ultimate goal of reading instruction.

THE ENGLISH ALPHABETIC WRITING SYSTEM

Many written languages use an alphabetic writing system where a letter or letters represent speech sounds called phonemes. To read, students must understand what is often called the *alphabetic principle*, or the idea that speech sounds or phonemes are represented by letters of the alphabet. This understanding is the same one that the early inventors of the alphabet used when creating the first alphabet thousands of years ago. Imagine early scribes thinking of individual sounds they heard in words or speech such as the sound /t/ and deciding to represent that sound in writing with the letter *t*.

English is an alphabetic writing system; however, unlike other alphabetic writing systems, the relationship between sounds and letters in English is a complex one. Other alphabets, for example, Spanish or Finnish, have a simple or transparent relationship between sounds or phonemes and symbols or letters, with one sound for one letter. In English there are approximately 44 speech sounds but only 26 letters; because of this, many English letters represent more than one sound and some letter pairs or letter combinations represent single or multiple sounds. To further complicate matters, the

English writing system is not only based on sound-symbol relationships, but it is also influenced by the origins of words and their meanings.

English spelling has been variously influenced by the Anglo-Saxon, French, Greek, and Latin languages. For example, in English, the /f/ in words of Greek origin is typically spelled *ph* (*photosynthesis, philanthropy*), and /er/ at the end of words derived from Latin is typically spelled *or* (*actor, director*). In another example of English spelling complexities, the words *lyre, lyric,* and *lyrical* share a common Greek root. Although the sound for the letter *y* changes in these words, the root and its meaning are preserved in English spellings, informing the reader that these words are related in meaning. The English alphabet has a deep-structured but largely regular spelling system, one that is based on sound, position, and meaning.

The role of the speech sound or phoneme is complicated in an alphabetic writing system and can make learning to read difficult for many early readers. Words are spoken so rapidly that it is difficult to divide them into individual speech sounds or phonemes. This is called *coarticulation*. Because it is hard to separate spoken words into phonemes, it is challenging to isolate and identify phonemes and match them to letters—the task required in early decoding and spelling and taught in early decoding instruction. Many phonemes are especially troublesome to identify, particularly when they occur in the middle or at the end of words. Some categories of phonemes are easily confused because they are so close in sound or the way they are produced in speech. Some phonemes distort the sounds or phonemes that are next to them in words, making the phoneme changeable, elusive, and hard to identify; this is called the *allophone* nature of the phoneme. All of these language-based issues make the identification and awareness of the phoneme, a central part of an alphabetic writing system and a necessary skill for early literacy acquisition, a significant challenge for many early readers.

TEACHING READING

Given the complexity of the language, teachers of reading must understand and teach the intricate structure of the English written language, including the alphabetic principle, to all students who are learning to read. Research from the U.S. and other countries shows there is consensus about the kind of instruction that works best for all children. The National Early Literacy Panel (NELP) published in 2009 in the U.S., analyzed research through meta-analysis (that is, statistical analysis of many research studies) to discover how early pre-reading skills develop in the beginning reader in preschool and kindergarten and which instructional techniques work best. The panel found six abilities in young children that strongly predicted successful early literacy skill development:

- alphabet knowledge
- phonological awareness
- rapid automatic naming of letters and digits
- rapid automatic naming of objects and colors
- writing or name writing
- phonological memory

NELP results further showed that successful, high-impact interventions that were most effective in promoting early literacy development were one-to-one or small group, occurred frequently during the school day, and were adult directed.

Prior to the NELP report, the Report of the National Reading Panel was published in 2000 in the United States. A panel of experts conducted a meta-analysis of decades of reading research studies and concluded that five component areas of reading instruction were needed:

- phonemic awareness
- phonics
- fluency
- vocabulary
- text comprehension

To ensure that school-aged students become efficient and effective readers, all of these five components must be explicitly taught in a systematic and structured way. Spelling and writing instruction are also important for all students learning to read and write.

Research from other countries confirms the findings of the U.S. Report of the National Reading Panel. Two international reports, *Teaching Reading: Report and Recommendations, National Inquiry into the Teaching of Literacy*, a research-based report from the Australian Government, dated December 2005, and *Independent Review of the Teaching of Early Reading*, an interim report from the United Kingdom, also dated December 2005, highlighted the need for effective practices in literacy instruction. These practices included the systematic teaching of phonics, which is central to understanding and mastery of any alphabetic writing system. The U.K. report emphasized the importance of effective teacher training and good teaching methods, stating, "We know that, to be effective, a high quality program must go hand in hand with high quality teaching." The Australian report called for effective initial instruction to reduce the amount of costly remedial programs. The Australian report also clearly endorsed the importance of direct, explicit instruction, ongoing assessment, and systematic and synthetic phonics instruction. The need for high-quality teacher training programs was also emphasized.

LEARNING TO READ

Many researchers have described the process of learning to read, generating models to illustrate this complicated process. In the 1980s, Dr. Jean Chall developed a theory of stages of reading development. Chall's beginning stages show the process of early literacy skill development, where a young reader gains the understanding that print imparts meaning. *Pre-Reading* is followed by *Initial Reading or Decoding*, as the reader demonstrates growing mastery of letter-sound relationships and high-frequency sight words. After this, the reader enters the stage of *Confirmation and Fluency*, where he or she gains automaticity and fluency, and later moves into the *Reading to Learn* stage. The final stages of Chall's model, *Multiple Points of View* and *Construction and Reconstruction*, depict the reader's developing ability to analyze text and generate new ideas.

Another helpful model, produced by Gough and Tunmer in 1986, portrays reading comprehension as a mathematical formula:

DECODING x LANGUAGE COMPREHENSION = READING COMPREHENSION

This model appears simple at first glance, but it is actually quite complex. It by no means implies that learning to read is a simple task. The *Simple View of Reading* formula shows the importance of accurate decoding in the reading process. It also takes into account the role of vocabulary and listening comprehension as it relates to reading comprehension. This formula demonstrates the relationship between the two components of reading comprehension—decoding and language comprehension. It is not merely a matter of adding these component skills together, but it is more like the process of multiplication, where each component influences the overall result. This formula also shows that each component is necessary but not sufficient alone for comprehension to occur. The student with dyslexia, for example, may have adequate listening comprehension but poor decoding, which often results in poor reading comprehension. When a passage is read aloud to this student he or she understands the material. When this student reads a similar passage, slow and labored decoding with impaired fluency often interfere with his or her reading comprehension in spite of adequate oral language comprehension.

Gough and Tunmer also note the close link between spoken and written language. The desire to be a reader is necessary but not sufficient for literacy development. Informed explicit and systematic instruction in phonemic awareness, phonics, fluency, vocabulary, and comprehension delivered by highly trained teachers who are knowledgeable about the structure of language is the key to unlocking the mysteries of the printed page.

2

THE PREVALENCE OF READING PROBLEMS AND DYSLEXIA

Many students struggle to learn to read and spell. In fact, learning disabilities are the most prevalent special education category and, further, dyslexia is the most common specific learning disability. Reading and spelling disorders remain prevalent despite recent trends and laws in education that focus on accountability and the need for research-based reading, spelling, and writing instruction. Dr. Pam Hook and Dr. Charles Haynes state, in *Reading and Writing in Child Language Disorders*, "The National Institutes of Health have recognized that high illiteracy rates are a national health care crisis that needs immediate attention. Approximately 10–15% of school-aged children have a learning disability, and of these, around 70% display disabilities specific to the literacy skills of reading and writing."

This crisis is demonstrated each year by the U.S. National Assessment of Educational Progress (NAEP), often called our Nation's Report Card, which consistently finds at least one third of all fourth grade students at the "Below Basic" level in reading and only one third of fourth grade students at or above proficient levels of reading. Additionally, NAEP data have continually demonstrated that the failure rate has been higher for some groups of students such as minority students, students living in poverty, and English Language Learners (ELL). For these students, the gap was huge, with approximately two thirds consistently obtaining below grade-level NAEP scores in reading.

It is true that reading failure is widespread. Yet, it is also true that effective early intervention, using research-based curriculum and instruction with a highly trained teacher, can prevent many early reading problems from becoming significant reading disorders. Teachers, pediatricians, and parents need to know what to look for so they can identify students early who are struggling to learn to read, before the gap between a student's progress and grade level becomes too wide. Decades of research have demonstrated that learning to read is a complex process and, despite motivation and instruction, many with average or above average intellectual abilities fail to achieve full literacy. Learning to read and spell is a language-based process, and many who struggle with literacy skills also struggle with other aspects of language skill development.

WHAT IS DYSLEXIA?

For more than a century, scientists have studied reading failure, beginning with studies of struggling readers. Reading disorders and reading failure are quite common; indeed, dyslexia is one of the most common and most carefully studied of all the learning disabilities, making up approximately 80% of diagnosed learning disabilities, according to Dr. Sally Shaywitz of Yale University, author of *Overcoming Dyslexia*. The word *dyslexia* literally means difficulties with (*dys/dis*) accessing the lexicon or writing system (*lexia*). In 2002, The International Dyslexia Association (IDA) defined dyslexia as follows:

> Dyslexia is a specific learning disability that is neurobiological in origin. It is characterized by difficulties in accurate and/or fluent word recognition and by poor spelling and decoding abilities. These difficulties typically result from a deficit in the phonological component of language that is often unexpected in relation to other cognitive abilities and the provision of effective classroom instruction. Secondary consequences may include problems in reading comprehension and reduced reading experiences that can impede the growth of vocabulary and background knowledge.

This definition is also used by the U.S. National Institutes of Child Health and Human Development (NICHD).

Understanding the definition of dyslexia helps parents and educators identify symptoms if they suspect a student may have this common reading disorder. The definition indicates that students with dyslexia have *poor decoding* or *poor single word reading* and they have *poor spelling* caused by *weak phonological processing*. This weak phonological processing can show up as difficulty pronouncing words, analyzing language, and learning and rapidly retrieving the names of objects, colors, numbers, letters, and letter sounds. *Phonological processing problems* refers to an inability to analyze language, resulting in difficulty segmenting speech into individual words, and later, dividing spoken words into syllables, and finally, separating spoken words into speech sounds or phonemes.

If a student has phonological *processing weaknesses, phonics* accuracy and automaticity, or learning sounds for a letter or group of letters, will be very difficult. Problems with *phonics* mastery cause *poor word reading or decoding,* which in turn have a negative impact on reading *fluency.* Weak reading *fluency* can cause problems with *reading comprehension.* Orthographic processing and mastering the English spelling system tends to lag behind. *Phonological problems* and *phonics difficulties* also cause *spelling problems,* which negatively affect writing skills. It is important to understand how these component skills affect one another and how one problem can lead to another: phonological weaknesses can cause a student to struggle with word reading, reading fluency, reading comprehension, spelling, and writing.

The definition of dyslexia also indicates that the disorder is *neurobiological* or brain-based. Since research has demonstrated that dyslexia is neurobiological or brain-based, there may be a family connection; research supports this claim, indicating that parents who have dyslexia have a higher incidence of children with this common disorder. Dyslexia may run in families; however, a family history of dyslexia is not a necessary characteristic for the diagnosis of dyslexia.

According to the definition, students with dyslexia may have had *effective classroom instruction* but still struggle with *reading* and *spelling* skill development. The performance of these students is often *unexpected in relation to other cognitive abilities* and other areas of achievement. In other words, in contrast with their weaknesses in learning to read, students with dyslexia often demonstrate real strengths in other areas such as math, drama, art, or science. While students with dyslexia are as smart or smarter than same-age peers, they have unanticipated difficulties learning to read due to language-based phonological weaknesses. This can be surprising since bright students would be expected to learn to read at an average rate. As you can imagine, seemingly capable and motivated students who are not reading and spelling well can puzzle parents, teachers, and the students themselves.

When students with weak phonological skills, poor decoding, and poor fluency struggle to learn to read, the process can be frustrating. The term *Matthew Effect* is used to describe what happens to these students. A student with poor phonological skills has difficulty identifying speech sounds or phonemes and matching sounds to print. Students with this profile have weak phonics skills, leading to poor decoding accuracy and weak reading fluency. If reading the words on the page is not accurate or fluent, reading comprehension often suffers. Without adequate decoding skills, the student reads poorly with little mastery, and this can lead to an avoidance of reading because without strong comprehension, reading is not rewarding.

When a student does not read an average amount, his or her vocabulary development often lags behind because vocabulary development comes largely from reading after the early elementary school years. To further compound the problem, a student who enters school with weak vocabulary and who does not learn to read is at risk for significant and cumulative academic difficulties.

Students who do not read well often become poor spellers and even poorer writers because strong spelling and writing skills depend upon strong reading skills. Students who struggle with orthographic memory can also have difficulty remembering spelling patterns and may have difficulty spelling high-frequency sight words such as *was* and *said*. Some students do better with reading but have significant problems with spelling and writing due to the complexities of the English spelling system and the demands it places upon orthographic memory.

Spelling and writing become increasingly important for academic achievement in the upper grades, and students who are weak readers, spellers, and writers frequently have related problems with schoolwork and homework completion. Students who have problems with reading and spelling can also experience secondary problems that include low self-esteem, stress, anxiety, somatic or health concerns, and, sometimes, emotional difficulties because school is difficult and work completion is problematic when you cannot read or spell well.

DYSLEXIA CAN BE MILD, MODERATE, OR SEVERE

Problems with reading, spelling, and writing can be mild, when the gap between the student's achievement and his or her grade level or intellectual potential is small. Reading problems such as dyslexia can also be moderate or severe when the gap between a student's achievement and grade level is significantly wider. When this occurs, a team of teachers and parents may refer the student for a comprehensive, clinical evaluation, also called in-depth diagnostic testing, to determine the student's present level of performance and to provide information to guide instruction.

TREATING DYSLEXIA WITH INSTRUCTION

Research has demonstrated that students with dyslexia who have early phonological problems and struggle with reading, spelling, and writing skills need specially designed instruction plus accommodations to the regular education program. The amount of specially designed instruction and type of modifications or accommodations to the regular education program that are needed are determined by diagnostically assessing a student's strengths and weaknesses. Assessment determines the weak areas that need further instruction; therefore, recommendations for specially designed instruction follow directly from weak areas identified in the testing. A comprehensive individual clinical assessment determines the student's present level of performance, finds areas of strength and weakness, and discerns whether a student's pattern of academic performance fits into a category appropriate for a diagnosis of a specific learning disability or specific learning disorder such as dyslexia.

SYMPTOMS OF DYSLEXIA OR READING PROBLEMS

Students with dyslexia are bright, with average or above average intellectual potential, and, as such, are aware that literacy skills are more challenging for them. They often feel discouraged, upset, and frustrated when reading acquisition is problematic and their skills lag behind those of their same-age peers.

Many students who are at risk for developing dyslexia show signs of language-based difficulties in preschool and kindergarten, including problems with expressive language, word pronunciation, and articulation. Students with dyslexia have difficulty with phonological skills such as rhyming, word pronunciation, and segmenting words into speech sounds or phonemes. They often have trouble learning names of letters or numbers and frequently have slow naming skills. They may also have slow expressive language production. Matching speech sounds or phonemes with letters or early phonics development is delayed. In kindergarten these students have problems decoding simple words such as *pat* and *mop*. Early spelling and writing is challenging when students have early reading problems.

In first and second grades, these students continue to struggle with phonological awareness and letter-sound relationships or phonics. Early decoding remains problematic, and they continue to struggle with spelling and writing skills. Handwriting can also be impaired as these students have difficulty learning letter names, matching the phoneme or speech sound to a letter or letters, and, then, cannot easily remember how to write the letters. When reading is challenging, spelling is even harder, and writing becomes most difficult.

For students in first, second, and third grade with weak reading skills, decoding accuracy is weak and reading is slow and effortful. Since mastery of decoding skills eludes these students, reading is a discouraging and unrewarding task. When decoding is not accurate and reading is not fluent, it is difficult to gain meaning from text and students become discouraged when they cannot make sense of what they are reading. Spelling and writing remain problematic.

Typically by third grade, average readers have mastered most phonics patterns in reading and spelling and are ready to read to learn. Students with dyslexia, however, may be reading below grade level, and when this occurs, all academic areas suffer. They continue to read inaccurately and slowly, to spell poorly, and to struggle with the complex demands of writing. Primary concerns with language and literacy can lead to secondary problems such as avoidance of reading and writing, school-related anxiety, health concerns, frustration, and work completion problems at home and at school. When students with dyslexia have not received adequate remediation, the student and parents struggle as academic demands increase.

In later elementary school, middle school, and high school, reading, spelling, and writing problems can become more pronounced as academic demands increase. Some students who have barely managed to get by may emerge with reading problems at this time as academic demands increase and their literacy skills cannot keep up. Others who have received remediation and are beginning to decode well remain slow readers who need accommodations. The most widely used accommodations are extended time together with a separate, quiet setting for testing. These accommodations help students who have low reading fluency and the difficulties caused by weak comprehension together with residual anxiety caused by literacy struggles. For older students with dyslexia, foreign language study is particularly challenging. Students with dyslexia who struggle to learn the phonemes in their native language have even more difficulty with phoneme awareness, speaking, decoding, and encoding in a second language.

Symptoms such as weak fluency and poor spelling often persist into adulthood. If reading and spelling skills are not mastered, older students and adults may struggle with academic and workplace demands. On the other hand, students who understand the nature of their dyslexia and can advocate for needed remediation and accommodations are very successful in their chosen endeavors. Most college and university programs offer support and accommodations to students with diagnosed dyslexia, and adults with diagnosed dyslexia can receive accommodations in the workplace. As stated by Louisa Moats and Karen Dakin in *Basic Facts About Dyslexia and Other Reading Disorders,* "A strong interest, hard work, and perseverance have carried many adults with dyslexia throughout the toughest period of their lives—school!—and enabled them to succeed in every possible walk of life."

U.S. FEDERAL LAW MANDATES SUPPORT FOR STUDENTS WITH DISABILITIES INCLUDING DYSLEXIA

According to federal law, dyslexia is a specific learning disability and, as such, it is covered in U.S. federal law written to mandate support for students with disabilities. All states must follow U.S. federal law to serve students with a disability or handicapping condition. Students with dyslexia are often referred to as students with a specific learning disability in reading, written language, or both areas, in public school settings. A specific learning disability is defined in the U.S. federal law (IDEIA 2004, 20 USC, Sec. 1401 (30) Specific Learning Disability) as follows:

> The term "specific learning disability" means a disorder in one or more of the basic psychological processes involved in understanding or in using language, spoken or written, which disorder may manifest itself in the imperfect ability to listen, think, speak, write, spell, or do mathematical calculations. The term includes such

conditions as perceptual disabilities, brain injury, minimal brain dysfunction, *dyslexia*, and developmental aphasia. Such term does not include a learning problem that is primarily the result of visual, hearing, or motor disabilities, of mental retardation, of emotional disturbance, or of environmental, cultural, or economic disadvantage.

The U.S. federal law also gives crucial information about the importance of effective instruction and its relationship to specific learning disabilities including dyslexia. It states that students who are learning English and struggle with reading are not necessarily students with a disability such as dyslexia. In 20 USC Sec. 1414 (b) (5), under the heading "Special Rules for Eligibility Determination," the law states:

> In making a determination of eligibility under paragraph (4) (A), a child shall not be determined to be a child with a disability if the determinant factor for such a determination is – (A) lack of appropriate instruction in reading, including the essential components of reading instruction (as defined in section 6368(3) of this title); (B) lack of instruction in math; or (C) limited English proficiency.

According to the most recent U.S. federal special education law, states must not require the use of the discrepancy formula (that is, finding a significant difference between cognitive or IQ scores and academic scores) to determine if a student has a specific learning disability. States and local school districts may consider whether there is a discrepancy, but according to federal law, they may not require it for identification of learning disabilities such as dyslexia. States and local school districts must take into account a student's response to intervention or response to instruction and other research-based measures to determine whether the student has a specific learning disability such as dyslexia. For years, professionals used the discrepancy formula to determine if a student had a specific learning disability. Decades of educational research have discredited this approach, and the 2004 U.S. federal law reflects new understanding of the importance of early intervention with expert instruction to catch students before they fall behind.

On the other hand, for students with complicated learning profiles, such as academically gifted students, the concept of an "unexpected gap" or discrepancy between aptitude and educational achievement can be very helpful in determining if a student has a co-occurring specific learning disability such as dyslexia and would need specially designed instruction and accommodations. Judicious use of the concept of discrepancy in combination with the student's response to intervention or instruction will yield a balanced approach to service delivery for students with diagnosed special learning needs.

Eligibility criteria for special education services and information about evaluation, assessment, and identification of specific learning disabilities, including dyslexia, are also found in the U.S. federal law:

IDEIA 2004

(6) Specific learning disabilities

(A) In general

Notwithstanding section 1406(b) of this title, when determining whether a child has a specific learning disability as defined in section 1401 of this title, a <u>local educational agency shall not be required to take into consideration whether a child has a severe discrepancy</u> between achievement and intellectual ability in oral expression, listening comprehension, written expression, basic reading skill, reading comprehension, mathematical calculation, or mathematical reasoning.

(B) Additional authority

In determining whether a child has a specific learning disability, a local educational agency may use a process that determines if the child responds to scientific, research-based intervention as a part of the evaluation procedures described in paragraphs (2) and (3).

§300.307 Specific learning disabilities.

(a) General. A State must adopt, consistent with §300.309, criteria for determining whether a child has a specific learning disability as defined in §300.8(c)(10). In addition, the criteria adopted by the State—

(1) Must not require the use of a severe discrepancy between intellectual ability and achievement for determining whether a child has a specific learning disability, as defined in §300.8(c)(10);

(2) Must permit the use of a process based on the child's response to scientific, research-based intervention; and

(3) May permit the use of other alternative research-based procedures for determining whether a child has a specific learning disability, as defined in §300.8(c)(10).

(b) Consistency with State criteria. A public agency must use the State criteria adopted pursuant to paragraph (a) of this section in determining whether a child has a specific learning disability.

(Authority: 20 U.S.C. 1221e-3; 1401(30); 1414(b)(6))

Dyslexia has been listed in federal documents under specific learning disabilities since the early 1960s and the word *dyslexia* was included in the first U.S. federal special education law, *Education for All Handicapped Children Act of 1975*, commonly called *Public Law 94-142*. All states must follow U.S. federal special education laws. Classification systems such as the *Diagnostic and Statistical Manual of Mental Disorders-5* (American Psychiatric Association) and *The International Classification of Diseases, 10th Revision (I.C.D.10*, World Health Organization) also provide information about specific learning disorders including disorders of reading and written language.

EARLY INSTRUCTION FOR STUDENTS WITH DYSLEXIA

The symptoms of language-based difficulties and literacy problems described earlier in the chapter provide clues for the parent and teacher, indicating that the child is struggling with early reading and spelling development. When a student is struggling with early literacy skills, a team approach is often used to gather evidence specific to each case. Teachers and parents can provide information about the student's language development, phonological awareness, and naming skills such as emerging letter name and letter sound knowledge. It is important to ask if there is a family history of reading and spelling problems, diagnosed or undiagnosed. Information gathered by the team can be useful in planning instruction.

It is essential to intervene early, taking advantage of brain plasticity, or the brain's ability to readily learn language, when students are young. When intervention is provided immediately with additional expert instruction at the first sign of language-based difficulties, the gap between a student's abilities and grade-level expectations is small. Kindergarten intervention studies support intervening early in the educational career, delivering additional research-based instruction in a developmentally appropriate way to students who are behind. A "wait-and-see" approach is not supported by the research; indeed, research has demonstrated that students who have early language-based difficulties and do not receive early intervention fall further behind. When this happens, the gap between their literacy skills and their grade level gets wider, making it even harder to catch up.

The U.S. federal law, with its references to a student's response to scientific, research-based intervention or instruction, supports an early or response-to-intervention approach. Many converging research findings show the importance of acting early, providing additional, research-based instruction for students who are falling behind in developing reading, spelling, and writing skills. Sadly, without early and effective intervention, studies indicate that three-fourths of students who are still behind in reading in third grade will remain behind through high school. This outcome can be avoided by providing expert instruction early in the educational career and monitoring progress to be sure interventions are closing the gap. As Louisa Cook Moats and Karen E. Dakin stress in *Basic Facts About Dyslexia and Other Reading Problems*, expert instruction is the treatment for dyslexia.

Understanding the warning signs that a student is struggling to develop early literacy skills helps with knowing when and how to provide help. Students with dyslexia need informed expert instruction in a research-based curriculum, provided by highly trained teachers with the correct, developmentally appropriate amount of instructional time.

Assessment helps to clarify whether a student is struggling with an area of academic skills and can provide clear recommendations for instructional support to remediate a learning problem. At-risk students who are identified early and receive additional literacy instruction can be successful, catch up to grade level, and go on to become accurate and fluent readers, spellers, and writers capable of understanding text and enjoying reading.

3

TYPES OF ASSESSMENT

Screening, Progress Monitoring, Outcomes, and Diagnostic

Ongoing assessment is critical for students acquiring reading skills as it opens the window into why students may be having difficulties as well as points the way to appropriate instruction. It is important to keep in mind that a major purpose for assessment is to aid in the development of curriculum and specific intervention strategies. In other words, assessment should drive instruction.

A well-integrated assessment for students who struggle with reading will indicate patterns in the test results that allow one to determine how reading performance is affected by both word identification skills and underlying oral language skills. For example, problems in reading comprehension can be due to various factors. In one instance, students with weak word identification may have trouble understanding a passage because they cannot figure out what the words are (difficulties with word identification). If they have strong listening comprehension skills, however, they do not have trouble understanding if the same passage is read to them. On the other hand, students with good word identification may have poor reading comprehension because of difficulties related to understanding the meaning of language. These comprehension difficulties are often apparent in listening tasks as well as when reading. For others, reading comprehension problems can be related to both word identification difficulties and general language comprehension issues. Other factors such as difficulties in organizing ideas, attention difficulties, and first language differences can also interfere with reading comprehension.

TYPES OF ASSESSMENT

To measure student performance appropriately, there are four general types of assessment that serve different purposes: *universal screening, progress monitoring, outcomes testing,* and *in-depth diagnostic testing.* Many tests, however, can be used for more than one purpose. Tests used for these purposes need to be valid, meaning that they are actually assessing the designated area. They also need to be reliable, meaning that the student would achieve a similar score if the test were given again by another person at a different time. These kinds of tests must be administered by individuals who are carefully trained in the specific administration requirements for each test.

In addition to establishing reliability and validity, some tests have been standardized using a representative national sample of the population. This means that these measures are designed to compare a specific student's performance to that of a student of the same age or in the same grade. Scores are obtained from samples of students that represent the U.S. population as a whole and are based on such factors as race and parental income. These kinds of tests are often referred to as "norm referenced" and allow comparison of scores across classes, ages, grades, and schools throughout the country. They result in scores such as standard scores and percentile ranks that compare a student's performance to the average. Standard scores that fall between 85 and 115 are generally considered to be within the average range. Analogous scores that are also often reported are percentile ranks where the average score ranges from the 16th percentile to the 84th percentile, which includes approximately 68% of the population. Percentile ranks indicate how many students perform above or below an individual student's score. (See Figure 1.) For example, if a student falls at the 45th percentile, that means approximately 55% of students of the same age (or grade) would perform better and 45% would perform worse on that

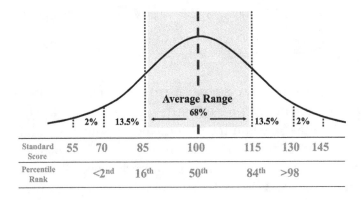

Figure 1. Interpretation of evaluation results: The bell curve.

particular assessment. Scores outside the average range indicate significant differences.

Other tests are designed to assess a student's performance
relative to a specific standard or *benchmark* that has been established as adequate for a certain point in the school year.
Typically, tests have established benchmarks for three points
in the year (beginning, middle, and end). Students can be
grouped for instruction according to their skill level relative
to this established benchmark. For example, the oral reading
fluency subtest of *Dynamic Indicators of Basic Early Literacy Skills
Next (DIBELS Next)* has established categories of performance
based on benchmarks for words per minute (wpm) across
the second grade year as shown in Table 1.

Table 1. Recommended Benchmark Goal Cut Point for Risk

	Core Instruction	Strategic	Intensive
Beginning of the year	80 wpm	55-7 wpm	< 55 wpm
Middle of the year	100 wpm	72-99 wpm	< 72 wpm
End of year	111 wpm	83-110 wpm	< 83 wpm

Most formal assessments use the national population
as the reference group but sometimes schools may develop
local norms based on the performance of students within
that school or district. There are also, however, informal and
criterion-referenced assessments that are designed to measure
specific skills knowledge. For example, it is important to assess
the words most frequently found in written text by grade level
beginning at kindergarten and moving through third grade.

These words are considered essential for children to be able to identify automatically and thus are taught directly. Periodic assessment of the student's ability to read these words quickly and accurately allows teachers or tutors to know which specific words still need to be addressed. Criterion-referenced tests are more informal and directly drive instruction.

Universal Screening

A universal screening for reading is usually administered to all children in a given grade at the beginning of the academic year and is designed to identify children who are at risk for reading failure. Results can be used to determine if a student is in need of extra instructional supports and additional assessment. The content of these screening measures differs depending on the grade of the children being assessed because the requirements for success in reading change as the child moves through the grades. For example, in kindergarten, it is important to screen for knowledge of the alphabet and the ability to hear sounds in words because these skills are predictive of how easily a child learns to read. A measure of vocabulary knowledge is often also included to estimate underlying oral language abilities that will be important for reading comprehension. Later, in third and fourth grade, speed of reading or fluency at the text level becomes critical as this is necessary for gaining information through reading. The importance of screening for reading comprehension also increases as students move through the grades. Because universal screening tests are given to all children, they are usually quick to administer and score. They are often group administered or individually administered in a short period of time.

An example of a group administered assessment that is used as a universal screening is the *Group Reading Assessment and Diagnostic Evaluation (GRADE)*. This test includes several subtests that measure performance in areas related to reading, such as listening comprehension, phonics, and silent reading comprehension. Standard scores and percentile ranks are available for this test and results can be used to determine which students are generally at risk in specific areas. This test is also often used at the end of the year as an outcomes measure to see how much progress a student has made compared to other students in the same grade.

An example of a frequently used individually administered screening test is *DIBELS Next*, mentioned before under benchmark testing. This test is quick to administer, requiring only about five minutes per child (although it may take somewhat longer in kindergarten and first grade where there are more subtests). *DIBELS Next* gives specific information about speed of processing as related to skills associated with strong oral reading fluency, such as letter naming, phonemic awareness, and non-word reading in kindergarten and oral reading of paragraphs in first through sixth grade. Results from this test can be used to determine which children are at risk for difficulties in reading acquisition and, thus, for forming initial instructional groupings at the beginning of the year. It also allows for continued quick assessments throughout the year as necessary to determine if specific instructional techniques are effective. (See Progress Monitoring below.)

Progress Monitoring

The second type of assessment is often called *progress monitoring* because it is given repeatedly throughout the year to ensure that adequate progress in reading growth is achieved. Again, the results of the progress monitoring should be used to plan instruction. As noted above, schools often do benchmark testing to monitor the progress of all students three times a year: at the beginning, in the middle, and at the end. The first administration serves as a screening measure, while the next two serve to determine if a student is continuing to struggle or is moving toward the specified benchmark. This kind of benchmark testing can be considered progress monitoring although some tests use the term *progress monitoring* only for further assessment that goes on in between these benchmark assessments. For students with a significant problem with reading acquisition, more frequent progress monitoring occurs—sometimes as often as weekly. This kind of progress monitoring data is critical for determining a student's response to intervention and, thus, whether or not a specific intervention is working. Examples of widely used progress monitoring tests that are linked to national norms are *DIBELS Next* for fluency as discussed earlier and *AIMSweb* for oral reading fluency and silent reading comprehension. The silent reading component of *AIMSweb* consists of graded paragraphs with every seventh word missing. The students read to themselves for three minutes and choose the correct word from a multiple choice. As with *DIBELS*, this assessment can be given three times a year as a benchmark and also in between for progress monitoring. Because this measure involves silent reading, it can be administered in small groups.

Outcomes

Outcomes assessment, the third type, is designed to evaluate overall reading achievement and usually occurs at the end of the year. These kinds of tests are usually norm referenced, standardized assessments and thus result in scores that allow students to be compared to other children of the same age or in the same grade to determine whether or not their reading skills fall within the average range. This information can be used to measure individual student success as well as performance of a class, grade, school, district, or state as a whole. Outcomes measures are often group administered achievement tests or high stakes tests designed at the state level. Some schools administer outcomes measures every year while others may only begin this kind of testing around second or third grade and administer these tests every two or three years.

Diagnostic

Finally, the fourth type of assessment, in-depth diagnostic assessment for reading, is often recommended after a trial period of intervention is not helping the student improve, and it is clear that the child is significantly struggling with acquisition of reading skills. Most often, it is through this kind of assessment that a diagnosis such as language-based learning disability, specific reading disability, or dyslexia can be determined and decisions can be made as to whether or not the child qualifies for special education services. Results are used to determine the at-risk student's specific patterns of strengths and weaknesses as well as his or her specific instructional needs. A diagnostic assessment includes a rather extensive battery of tests that is individually administered and requires lengthy testing sessions. This in-depth testing can sometimes be completed through the school, or it is administered by an outside evaluator or clinic.

When Diagnostic Testing Is Indicated

Diagnostic assessment should aid in the development of curricula and intervention strategies. When reading development is not responding adequately to intervention it is important to evaluate skills in critical areas related to listening, speaking, reading, and writing.

Because reading is based on the oral language system, the battery of tests should generally include assessment in the areas of oral language comprehension and use if there is any concern about an underlying oral language difficulty. This type of testing is done by a certified speech-language pathologist.

Underlying processing and memory skills including phonological awareness, phonological memory, and rapid automatic naming, as well as specific areas directly related to reading, spelling, and writing should be standard to any battery. It is important that both accuracy and speed of reading be measured as some students read accurately but very slowly and with great difficulty. It is also necessary to evaluate reading of single real words and non-words as well as sentences and paragraphs. Both oral and silent reading should be assessed in that some students struggle to a greater degree with one or the other.

This type of testing must be administered by highly trained professionals and is often completed by a team consisting of specialists in reading, speech/language pathology, and educational psychology. Evaluations done outside of the school setting are often completed by cognitive neuropsychologists or educational psychologists.

All of this information should be combined with classroom observation and information about the student's cognitive

abilities as well as medical, behavioral, social, and cultural
factors to create a complete profile for the individual student.
Any other academic areas in which the student struggles,
such as math, should also be evaluated. Often difficulties in
math stem from reading problems, particularly in the upper
grades as word problems become more common.

Choosing an Effective and Efficient Assessment Battery

Assessment must be effective in identifying children in
need but also efficient so that it is not too time consuming
and does not significantly reduce actual instructional time.
Some of the considerations that arise when choosing an
assessment battery are the following characteristics:

- individual, small group, or large group testing
- timed or untimed
- formal or informal
- standardized or skills based

Each type of assessment has pros and cons. For example,
large group testing is the most efficient in that many students
can be tested at the same time. However, it may not be as
effective for those students who have trouble paying attention
in larger groups, such as young children in kindergarten and
first grade or students at any age with attention issues that
interfere with focusing and following directions. Also, certain
skills can be measured individually or in groups, for example,
silent reading. Other skills may require an oral response and,
thus, can only be administered individually.

Whether or not a test is timed or untimed can also affect a student's performance. Some students are slower in

processing and responding and thus do more poorly under timed conditions. On the other hand, it is essential to assess speed of processing through administering timed tests because some students score within the average range with unlimited time, thus masking fluency problems. Again, sometimes an informal test gives more information than a formal standardized test about specific content knowledge but does not allow for comparison of that student to others relative to national norms. Within a well-designed assessment battery, there is usually a need for many different kinds of measures to get a complete picture of a student's individual pattern of strengths and areas of need.

4

CLINICAL
EVALUATION
OF DYSLEXIA

Sometimes an individual clinical evaluation is needed to determine if a student has a specific learning disability or other condition that affects learning. U.S. federal law supports an early intervention approach called *response to intervention* so that students do not fall far behind before they are found eligible for special or additional instruction. Using a response-to-intervention approach, school teams provide research-based instruction and regularly scheduled progress monitoring to closely watch all students' progress. When individual students do not make adequate yearly progress, it is important to gather information to help with program planning and instructional support for that student. Assessment is a vitally important part of that process.

Research on reading development and effective instruction provides consensus that instruction in the five components of reading—phonemic awareness, phonics, fluency, vocabulary, and comprehension—plus spelling, writing, and language development is important for all students. For decades, research has confirmed that these skills should be taught directly, systematically, and explicitly with appropriate intensity of instruction and sufficient practice, so all students attain mastery. Research on early literacy skill development in kindergarten and even at the preschool level shows that the earlier the intervention occurs when students are struggling the better the outcomes; a "wait-and-see approach" when students are struggling leads to those students falling further behind.

Early intervention should be developmentally appropriate, providing instruction and frequent distributed practice or mini-lessons taught throughout the school day in component skills that are necessary to support early literacy skill development. Information from brain research has demonstrated that the brain is especially plastic-like for learning language at early ages; because of brain plasticity, students can catch up more readily and master language-based skills when teachers intervene early with appropriate instruction and when the gap is narrow between students' skills and average, grade-level skills. Decades of research on retention has indicated that holding students back and repeating grades does not remediate or help students who have learning disabilities. Research indicates that the most common learning disability is dyslexia or a problem with reading and spelling. To quote Louisa C. Moats and Karen E. Dakin in *Basic Facts About Dyslexia and Other Reading Problems*, when students have dyslexia or reading problems, "Expert teaching is the treatment; dyslexia treatment is educational."

HOW IS DYSLEXIA ASSESSED?

The definition of dyslexia discussed in Chapter 2 is a helpful tool for thinking about what to assess because it describes the key features or symptoms of dyslexia. These symptoms (in italics in the definition below) and how they can be assessed are discussed in more detail in the section that follows.

> **Dyslexia** is a specific learning disability that is *neurobiological* in origin. It is characterized by difficulties in *accurate and/or fluent word recognition* and by *poor spelling* and *decoding* abilities. These difficulties typically result from a *deficit in the phonological component of language* that is often *unexpected in relation to other cognitive abilities* and *the provision of effective classroom instruction.* Secondary consequences may include *problems in reading comprehension* and *reduced reading experiences* that can impede the growth of *vocabulary and background knowledge.*

The symptoms of dyslexia described in the definition are very specific. To determine if a student has dyslexia, each of the symptoms in italics in the above definition should be carefully considered and several components should be directly evaluated.

WHAT AREAS SHOULD BE TESTED IN A CLINICAL EVALUATION OF DYSLEXIA?

Neurobiological Differences

A large body of research shows that people with dyslexia have neurobiological or brain-based differences and language-based differences that are not related to cognitive abilities or intelligence. This common problem with word reading and spelling, with its phonological core deficit, has been carefully studied by brain researchers and other scientists. Asking whether there is a family history of problems with speech and language, reading, and spelling and writing development on intake forms may provide helpful information.

Word Recognition

Accurate and fluent word recognition is a core problem for individuals with dyslexia. Assessment should include measures of how *accurately* an individual can read words as well as how *fluently* words can be read. To measure accuracy of word reading, students are asked to read aloud lists of words that are typically read by students at different grade levels. Word lists can be composed of real words or nonsense words. Nonsense words follow English spelling patterns. Reading nonsense words shows how well the student has mastered phonics skills or sound-symbol knowledge, which can indicate how well a student can read an unknown word.

Depending on the type of test used, the level can be expressed in a variety of ways such as a standard score, a percentile rank, or an age or grade level. To measure the *fluency* of word recognition, the focus is on how quickly and accurately students recognize and read words either in word lists or in connected text. Students are asked to read as many words as possible within a time frame (for example, within one minute) and the number of words read correctly per minute is calculated. Scores are compared to norms showing what is expected for students at different age or grade levels.

Spelling

Poor spelling can also be a symptom of dyslexia. Spelling is measured by asking individuals to spell a variety of types of words with varying phonics patterns, words containing the six syllable types in English, words illustrating common spelling rules and patterns, and words with irregular spelling patterns. The type of spelling errors made by the student should be analyzed and described. The analysis of a student's spelling errors indicates which phonics patterns and orthographic patterns the student does not know. This analysis leads to recommendations for specially designed instruction or remediation targeted to meet that student's spelling needs.

Decoding

Decoding refers to the ability to read familiar and unfamiliar words by using the individual's knowledge of the letters and letter patterns that are used to represent sounds in the English language. Assessment should include information about the sound-symbol associations the student has learned as well as how the student uses this information to read words that are unknown. Students are typically shown letters, consonants, and vowels that are used to spell the common sounds in English words and are asked to give the sounds that the letters represent. For example, the student would be shown the letters *ay* and asked to give the sound these letters would make in a word. In addition, the student is shown *made-up* or *nonsense* words and asked to read them. These words follow English spelling patterns but are not real words, for example, *nish* and *barth*. Such words can only be read by decoding, using phonics-based knowledge.

Phonological Processing

Research has clearly established that the cause of the reading and spelling problems for individuals with dyslexia is a deficit in the phonological component of language. This symptom is often referred to as the *phonological core deficit* in research about reading disorders and dyslexia. A thorough assessment of dyslexia should include measures of the three phonological processing skills—phonological awareness, phonological memory, and rapid automatic naming—that are known to be related to word reading, spelling, and decoding difficulties. A common area of phonological processing difficulty is phonological awareness, but many students also have problems in rapid naming and phonological memory. Individuals with problems or weaknesses in two or three of these phonological skills have been shown to have more difficulty learning to read than students with a deficit in only one area of phonological processing.

Phonological Awareness

This language-based ability to segment speech into words, syllables, and phonemes is vitally important for literacy skill development and supports decoding and encoding or spelling abilities. Phonological awareness skills require the conscious awareness that spoken language can be broken into parts: words, syllables, onsets (the sound or sounds before the vowel) and rimes (the word families or vowel and ending sounds), and phonemes. These skills range from very simple tasks that most preschoolers can easily do (for example, clap for each word in a spoken sentence or clap for each syllable in a spoken word) to the skills required to analyze the individual sounds within spoken words (for example, say the word *clean* without saying the /l/ sound: "keen").

Phonemic awareness is the ability to identify and manipulate speech sounds or phonemes in spoken words. Phonemic awareness is causally related to reading skill development; understanding that words are made up of speech sounds or phonemes and manipulating those speech sounds or phonemes supports phonics or sound-symbol relationships that are central to early decoding and reading mastery. Problems or weaknesses in phonemic awareness are a cause of dyslexia or difficulties with early decoding and reading skill development.

The good news is that phonemic awareness skills can be improved by direct, explicit, and systematic instruction. Improvements in phonemic awareness cause improvements in reading skills. Assessment in phonemic awareness should specify how the student is performing with the development of phonological skills compared to the average for the student's age and grade. Once a student's level of phonological skills is determined, instructional planning can begin. Research-based curriculum links phonological awareness with phonics, decoding, and encoding or spelling instruction.

Phonological Memory

Also called verbal short-term memory, phonological memory is the ability to hold verbal information in short-term memory. The best example is the ability to hold a string of numbers, such as a telephone number, in short-term memory until the numbers can be written down. The terms *phonological* and *verbal* indicate that the information being held in memory involves the sounds of words or language-based information rather than a picture or design. The ability to hold information in short-term memory is important because it is the first step in placing information in long-term memory so that it can be recalled later.

Difficulties in phonological memory can have an impact on several aspects of reading. For example, a student may be able to segment a word into five or six sounds but then cannot remember all of the sounds to blend them into the correct word. Students may have difficulty holding information that is read (or read to them) in their memory long enough to thoroughly process and understand the meaning. Difficulty holding the sounds of words in short-term memory can also make it hard for students to develop the vocabulary necessary for strong reading comprehension and successful spelling. To test phonological memory, individuals are often asked to repeat strings of numbers or unfamiliar, nonsense words.

Rapid Automatic Naming (RAN)

RAN tests measure how quickly an individual can name items such as colors, objects, letters, and numbers and are designed to be indicators of problems in a variety of phonological skills that are related to the development of reading. The ability to quickly name things is related to a student's ability to develop automaticity in reading subskills such as quickly recalling the sounds that are represented by letters and strings of letters. Students can have deficits on RAN tests for a variety of reasons, but one of the most common reasons is a general difficulty in rapidly retrieving the name or label of an item. One of the things that students must learn early in reading development is the names of items such as letters. For young students, letters are abstract visual symbols and their "names" bear no relationship to the visual representations. To make matters more complicated, letters have "names" and letters also have one or more "sounds." Difficulty retrieving those labels quickly, which is referred to as a *word retrieval* or *naming* problem, has significant implications for instruction. Depending on the severity of the word retrieval problem, a student may have difficulty initially learning letter names and letter sounds that are important for reading. Even after the student has learned letter-sound associations and common high-frequency words, reading may be slow and effortful. Such students are often described as "knowing a word one day and not the next" and for them, reading is a frustrating task. Students with RAN difficulties often have problems with reading fluency. The combination of weak phonological skills and rapid naming is often called a *double deficit* in literature about reading disorders and dyslexia.

Reading Comprehension

It is widely accepted that good comprehension is the goal of all reading instruction and, indeed, it is the purpose of reading. Reading comprehension tests measure a student's understanding of material read. A student's comprehension should be assessed at the sentence level and at the paragraph level because most material read by older students is at the paragraph level and beyond. Tests of reading comprehension require a student to read silently or aloud, then answer questions presented orally by the examiner or choose answers presented in a multiple choice format. Some assessment measures ask students to write answers to questions posed, combining the tasks of reading, spelling, and writing in the subtest design.

OTHER IMPORTANT AREAS OF ASSESSMENT TO CONSIDER

Oral Language

As noted in previous chapters, oral language is the foundation for reading and writing. Thus, any difficulties in either listening comprehension or the ability to express ideas orally will certainly interfere with literacy skill development, particularly with reading comprehension and written expression. For students who seem to struggle with oral language, an evaluation in that area is needed. It is important to assess both understanding, or receptive language, and the use of oral or expressive language as students may differ in these two areas. Difficulties with oral language comprehension will affect reading comprehension while difficulties in oral expression may have more of an effect on writing. This evaluation should be completed by a certified speech and language pathologist as a member of the assessment team.

The assessment should include a measure of vocabulary comprehension because vocabulary knowledge is highly correlated with reading comprehension. Other areas affect students' comprehension and are more difficult to assess with standardized test measures. These include aspects of language related to grammar or syntax and morphology, or meaningful parts of words, as well as correct intonation and rhythm while reading. Higher-order thinking skills (that is, the ability to think abstractly about the meaning of language) are also essential for strong comprehension. For example, understanding how two concepts are related or the ability to find the main idea, draw inferences, and summarize are important for skilled reading comprehension. Students who struggle in these areas often have trouble "reading between the lines"; they can read the words and understand the literal meaning but have difficulty with reasoning or comprehending what they are reading. These language abilities become more important as children move up through the grades as by grade four children are "reading to learn" rather than "learning to read." Interestingly, problems in these areas also show up in students' writing.

Information about oral language can also be gained from the intelligence testing that can be part of an evaluation for dyslexia. A commonly used assessment tool is the *Wechsler Individual Intelligence Test—Fourth Edition (WISC-IV)*. The *WISC-IV* contains an index called the Verbal Comprehension Index, which has three subtests: Vocabulary, Similarities, and Comprehension. Performance on these measures can give insight into vocabulary knowledge and verbal reasoning skills and does not require any reading. It is important to understand, however, that sometimes these scores are lowered by the fact the student has to use language to explain his or her answers. For example, on the Vocabulary subtest, the word must be defined; whereas, in a commonly administered vocabulary test often given by the speech-language pathologist or diagnostician, the child can point to a picture to indicate whether or not the word is understood. Here, it is important to determine whether there is a significant difference between the ability to understand language (*receptive*) and the ability to use it (*expressive*). All of the subtests on the *WISC-IV* Verbal Comprehension Index require that answers be explained verbally and questioned if they are low. Low scores on this index indicate the need for a more in-depth evaluation of oral language by a speech-language pathologist.

Finally, a thorough history of the student's speech and language development should be taken, and any prior evaluations of speech and language should be considered as part of the student's educational history during the evaluation and re-evaluation processes. Because dyslexia and specific reading disabilities are language-based disorders, often the first symptoms or weaknesses are seen in the area of the child's speech and language development.

Visual/Orthographic Processing

Although the definition of dyslexia focuses on the importance of phonological processing skills, research and clinical observation make it clear that some students also have great difficulty developing the orthographic skills necessary for accurate and efficient reading and spelling. Orthographic memory is important for reading and spelling mastery. While English is a complicated alphabetic writing system, research shows the spelling of most English words follow reliable rules. With the provision of high quality instruction, students with adequate orthographic processing can learn to rapidly and accurately read and spell words that follow orthographic rules.

Students with weak orthographic processing skills struggle to develop automaticity with reading and spelling. Words with irregular spelling patterns that do not follow the rules of English present an even greater challenge for students with poor orthographic processing skills. These words include many high-frequency words, such as *come, want, does,* and *was,* whose spelling patterns are not regular and whose automatic recognition is critical for reading. Another challenge is presented by words that sound the same but have different meanings based on their spellings. Examples include *read* and *reed*, *their* and *there*, and *birth* and *berth*. For these words and irregular words, good phonemic awareness skills and knowledge of sound-symbol associations or phonics are not sufficient. The student must remember or recognize the specific string of letters that is appropriate for each word. Skill in this area is typically evaluated by asking the individual to spell and read words with irregular patterns.

Mathematical Skills

Math skills are typically tested as part of the educational assessment when the student has suspected dyslexia or reading problems. Language problems can cause difficulties with the understanding of math word problems; additionally, decoding or word reading difficulties can make math word problems very challenging for the student with dyslexia. Students with weak RAN, weak rapid retrieval of verbal information, or problems with verbal fluency can have difficulties with mathematical fluency. Math fluency can also be weak in students who have language-based weaknesses and phonological memory difficulties. It is important to note that these math fluency problems can be separate from and are often significantly lower than a student's math calculation or math reasoning skills. Some students are at or above grade level in math calculation and math reasoning, but they have very weak math fluency requiring the accommodation of extended time to give them the time needed to show what they know.

The clinician should conduct a comprehensive assessment of mathematical skills and then conduct a careful analysis of a student's performance and answers to determine the individual pattern of strengths and weaknesses. It is important to look closely at math subtest scores to tease out these issues because a broad or overall math score can mask serious problems with components of math skills. It is also important to analyze a student's math errors to determine what to teach or re-teach. A skilled diagnostician can interpret these subtests and provide recommendations for remediation and accommodations based upon a student's individual profile of strengths and weaknesses. Providing a comprehensive assessment and interpretation of a student's math skills provides assurance that the student is placed in the appropriate math group and math courses.

ASSESSMENT OF DYSLEXIA — A COMPONENT-BASED APPROACH

To review, an evaluation for dyslexia should include the following tests and assessments:

- test phonological processing, including
  - phonological awareness
  - phonological or language-based memory
  - rapid automatic naming (RAN)
- take a family history of reading or spelling problems
- ask about the student's birth, developmental, family, and school history
- assess decoding, or single word reading, and spelling
- test specifically for dyslexia by
  - measuring oral reading of single words and nonsense words and
  - assessing oral reading in the context of sentences and paragraphs

- test reading comprehension, using passages longer than sentence level

- assess the student's receptive vocabulary

- assess the student's skill in spelling single words and assess spelling in the context of sentence and paragraph writing

- assess writing skills beyond the sentence level (because paragraph and essay writing skills become increasingly important as students advance in grades)

- assess mathematical ability in the areas of untimed calculations, mathematical reasoning (word problems read aloud to the students), and mathematical fluency (because some students with language-based problems struggle with mathematical fluency and poor readers struggle to decode mathematical word problems)

A component-based assessment such as this uses the definition of dyslexia to guide assessment. This approach considers the symptoms of dyslexia and assesses whether the student has symptoms that are characteristic of the disorder. Cognitive or intelligence testing can be an important part of the assessment battery and is vital for students with complicated learning profiles such as twice exceptional students, those with superior cognitive skills who also have reading problems.

WHO TESTS FOR DYSLEXIA?

Psychologists at the masters or doctoral level can assess specific learning disabilities, including reading disorders, language-based learning disorders, and dyslexia. Reading specialists or educational diagnosticians with advanced degrees at the masters or doctoral level who have completed assessment coursework and who have expertise in clinical and educational assessment are also qualified to make these assessments. To administer standardized tests, professionals must have completed a course in tests and measurements, which is usually part of a graduate-level program. Tests and measurement courses cover aspects of clinical assessment, including reliability, validity, standardization, and data analysis. Graduate students in assessment courses study actual test instruments and then give test batteries under supervision. Coursework and supervision in test scoring, test interpretation, and report writing are part of a good, rigorous clinical program at the graduate school level.

Completing coursework, including clinical supervision, ensures that graduate-level students master clinical and professional ethical issues relative to assessment of human subjects. Clinical coursework also includes supervision in data analysis, making diagnoses when appropriate, generating recommendations for specially designed instruction and accommodations to the regular education program, and presenting results of evaluations to parents and other professionals. Supervision ensures that skills in these sensitive areas are mastered. Persons who lack appropriate professional credentials and who have not had clinical coursework may not purchase or administer standardized tests; professional and ethical issues govern the purchase and use of standardized tests. Additionally, only licensed psychologists (in some states, educational diagnosticians) are authorized to give cognitive or intelligence tests, and for many students this type of testing is an essential part of the assessment battery, providing valuable information about aspects of cognitive functioning.

When a student is struggling academically and parents and teachers continue to wonder if the student has a learning disability, it is essential to refer him or her for evaluation. Educational specialists, reading specialists, or psychologists who are well versed in the process of learning to read and assessment of reading disorders provide the "trained eye" needed to spot students who are experiencing difficulties with literacy skill development. Experienced clinicians use reliable and valid standardized test instruments to ensure that the evaluation is objective and provides the best information. Assessment and diagnosis becomes an important part of a student's academic record because it documents the presence of a disability and provides valuable information about student achievement and progress.

As students advance in their educational careers, moving from elementary to high school and into colleges or universities, they need updated assessment reports that provide documentation of educational history and diagnosis of disorders, such as learning disabilities and dyslexia, for eligibility into programs providing support and accommodations at schools, colleges, and universities. Some adults with dyslexia need updated assessments to document the presence of their learning disability and provide evidence to support requests for accommodations in the workplace. Assessment of dyslexia is vitally important throughout a person's educational and professional career, providing needed information about the presence of this most common learning disorder. Individuals with dyslexia who understand the nature of their diagnosis can become successful self-advocates who obtain needed remediation and accommodation as required.

5

LINKING ASSESSMENT TO INSTRUCTION

Recommendations for Educational Programming

Assessment drives or informs instruction by determining the *nature* and *severity* of the reading problem. Both of these factors vary greatly in students diagnosed with dyslexia, so they must be carefully assessed to determine the best treatment or course of instruction.

NATURE OR TYPE OF PROBLEM

Individuals with dyslexia may have a deficit in one or more of the phonological processing skills that are important for reading. The most common area of phonological processing difficulty is phonological awareness but many students also have problems in rapid naming and phonological memory (See Chapter 2 for more information). In addition, some individuals have a specific problem involving orthographic processing. Individuals with problems in more than one type of processing skill have been shown to have more difficulty learning to read than students with a deficit in only one area. The type of reading problem can also vary. One student may have a problem only in the accuracy of word reading while another student may have problems in accuracy as well as automaticity of word recognition (that is, how quickly words can be identified).

SEVERITY OR DEGREE OF PROBLEM

Individuals with dyslexia can have relatively mild to very severe problems in phonological processing as well as in different aspects of reading and writing. For example, a student with mild to moderate difficulty in phonological awareness may respond quickly to appropriate instruction in this area. However, if this same student also has a severe problem in the area of rapid naming, learning skills such as letter-sound associations, spelling patterns, and sight words may be very difficult and require extensive interventions over a long period of time.

A detailed assessment also provides what is referred to in the development of an Individualized Education Program (IEP) as a "present level of performance." A comprehensive description of the nature and severity of the student's reading, writing, and phonological processing difficulties is essential for developing an appropriate IEP. In addition, the assessment information can also be used as a baseline (beginning point) for determining whether or not the student shows improvement in response to instruction.

With information in hand concerning the nature and degree of difficulties a student has in reading and phonological and orthographic processing, the next step is to link this information to appropriate instruction. Appropriate instruction must include *what* is taught as well as *how* each student is taught. Fortunately, an abundance of information is available from research about the characteristics of instruction that are effective with students who struggle with reading.

CHARACTERISTICS OF EFFECTIVE INSTRUCTION

In Chapter 1, the characteristics of effective instruction were described based on the findings of several research-based reports. The characteristics supported by numerous studies from around the world include both the *how* and *what* of effective literacy instruction. A clear consensus supports the areas of phonemic awareness, phonics, fluency, vocabulary, and text comprehension as the basis of *what* should be taught. As to *how* these areas should be taught, research supports the use of instruction that is explicit, direct, systematic, supportive, multisensory, and research based. Other important factors include the intensity and fidelity of instruction, the use of assessment to guide instruction, differentiation of instruction to meet individual needs, and teaching to mastery.

The following research findings describe what is known about *how* instruction should be delivered to be effective for students with dyslexia.

How to Teach

Explicit, Direct, and Systematic Instruction

Instruction that is explicit, direct, and systematic leaves nothing to chance. *Systematic* instruction teaches skills in a specific order based on moving from simple to more complex information. Each skill is taught *explicitly* and clearly and students are not expected to figure out critical information on their own. Instruction is provided in *different* ways to meet the specific needs of individual students and students are *supported* at each step of the process. Both emotional and cognitive supports are important for students with more severe reading problems. Emotional support involves positive reinforcement and encouragement. Students who have experienced failure must be shown that they can be successful. Cognitive support requires careful scaffolding of instruction including gradual introduction of skills with review and practice before new skills are introduced. Teachers must be adept at diagnosing the precise type of instruction each student needs at each point in the process and skills must be taught to mastery (until they are truly automatic).

Multisensory Instruction

Instruction that is *multisensory* engages students in activities that involve multiple pathways of learning in the brain. The term *VAKT* refers to the simultaneous use of visual, auditory, kinesthetic, and tactile responses to enhance memory and learning. This type of instruction, which is also explicit, systematic, and cumulative, is referred to as *multisensory structured language education* (MSLE). In MSLE, reading skills are taught using both synthetic (part to whole) and analytic (whole to part) methods.

Intensity of Instruction

Instructional *intensity* can be provided in several ways, including the size of the reading group, the amount of time the student receives instruction, the frequency of instruction, the training of the teacher, and the program or materials being used for instruction. Instruction must be intensive enough so that students make steady progress toward the goal of catching up with their peers in terms of reading skills. To catch up, students must make more than one year's progress in basic reading for each year of instruction.

For example, if an average of 80 minutes of daily instruction is required for normal growth, a fifth grader who is three years behind needs 80 additional minutes each day for catch-up growth. To catch up in two years (by the end of seventh grade) would require 200 minutes of reading instruction daily. Of course, this is simply an approximation based on average data but the point is that catch-up growth requires additional time spent in the appropriate type of reading instruction. For students with dyslexia, this means instruction that teaches them the basic reading skills in which they are deficient (that is, remedial instruction) as well as instruction that teaches them the grade-level skills that their peers are learning.

Catch-up is easiest in the early grades and becomes more difficult with each passing year, but it is never too late! Even though some students with extremely severe reading problems may never reach the 50th percentile levels of reading skill, all students can make steady improvements over time with appropriate instruction.

Fidelity of Instruction

Programs and materials must be used with *fidelity*. Implementing reading programs and materials that are based on sound research is critical but not sufficient for the success of students with dyslexia. Fidelity of instruction requires that the materials be used in the manner that they were intended (for example, all steps in the selected program must be taught daily) and taught by teachers who have specific training in using the materials appropriately. Fidelity of instruction should be monitored and documented, and teachers should be supported within their school system to ensure that programs are implemented correctly.

What to Teach and Why

The current definition of dyslexia emphasizes the importance of deficits in the phonological component of language as the basis for the reading and spelling problems that characterize dyslexia. These phonological processing components include phonological awareness, phonological memory, and rapid naming. In addition, as discussed earlier, deficits in orthographic processing in an evaluation of a student's reading disorder are important. Before discussing the reading and spelling skills that should be taught, it is important to review the implications for instruction related to the type and degree of *processing* problems.

Phonological Awareness Instruction

Phonological awareness is an umbrella term that includes skills ranging from very simple tasks that most preschoolers can easily do (for example, clap for each word in a spoken sentence) to the skills required to analyze the individual sounds within spoken words (for example, say the word *smash* without saying the /m/ sound: "sash"). Phonological awareness skills require the conscious awareness that spoken language can be broken into parts (that is, words, syllables, onsets and rimes, and phonemes). Although each of these levels of analysis is important, for most students who are diagnosed with dyslexia, the critical component is their ability to analyze the individual sounds (or phonemes) of words. Assessment should specify exactly where on the spectrum of phonological awareness skills the student is performing and how severe the problem is at that level. For example, a third grader who can successfully segment words into syllables and give the beginning sound in words is clearly functioning at the phoneme level of phonological awareness. This level, also referred to as *phonemic awareness,* is the level that must be reached before students can learn to read and spell using the sounds and letters of English. It is not sufficient, however, to know that this third grader has reached the phoneme level; assessment must also specify which phoneme-level skills have been mastered. Before planning instruction, it is important to know if the student can *identify* all of the sounds within words (for example, say each sound within a word of five to six sounds) as well as *analyze* sounds within words to make changes (for example, change the word *rap* to *trap* to *tap* and explain the changes). Only after the details of the student's phonological awareness skills are identified, can instruction be focused appropriately.

Phonological awareness instruction is most effective when it focuses primarily on segmenting and blending activities and teaches students about the sounds of language in combination with letters as soon as possible. Instruction should be systematic and explicit, and skills should be taught in a sequence from simple to complex. For students with dyslexia, instruction should focus on the phoneme level as quickly as possible but simpler levels of instruction may be necessary for younger students or those with more severe problems.

Phonemic awareness skills should not be taught in isolation but should be explicitly linked to reading and spelling. An example of this is teaching students to segment spoken words into individual sounds by tapping each sound with their fingers before spelling the words using letters. This strategy explicitly focuses the student's attention on the individual sounds within spoken words that must be mapped onto individual letters or letter patterns for accurate spelling.

Phonological Memory Instruction and Support

The term *phonological memory* (also called *verbal short-term memory*) refers to the ability to hold verbal information in short-term memory. The information being held in verbal short-term or phonological memory is language-based and involves the sounds of words. After information is held in verbal short-term or phonological memory it can be placed into long-term memory for later recall. Students with phonological memory problems can have significant difficulties with reading. They may be able to segment words into sounds but have trouble blending all the sounds together to make a word, resulting in slow and dysfluent reading. When students with phonological memory problems listen to a story or hear lengthy verbal directions, they may have difficulty holding all the information in short-term memory and working with the information presented. Comprehension and even vocabulary development may suffer when verbal short-term memory or phonological memory is impaired. Memorization and immediate recall of language-based information such as multiplication tables in math or lists of content area information may be challenging for students with impaired phonological memory.

If students have deficits in this area, a useful approach is to teach them strategies that help them compensate for their difficulties. An example is teaching a student to organize information into manageable chunks rather than try to hold a number of individual items in memory. For reading and spelling individual words, this can be accomplished by teaching students to divide words into parts such as the onset and rime. Teaching students to recognize patterns within words, such as prefixes, suffixes, and syllables, is also an excellent strategy. In reading text, students can be taught strategies such as simple note taking and frequent pausing when reading to help them answer questions about or to paraphrase what has been read.

Rapid Automatic Naming (RAN) Instruction and Support

RAN tests measure rapid naming of items, colors, numbers, and letters and this language-based skill is closely linked to reading skill development. Problems with rapid automatic naming or retrieval are a marker for a reading problem and can indicate the likelihood of difficulties with reading fluency. Students who struggle with RAN often have problems learning letter names, matching letter names with letter sounds, and with early phonics mastery and automaticity. Problems in this area can be mild, moderate, or severe. When problems with RAN are combined with other phonological deficits such as a lack of phonemic awareness or weak phonological memory, students can be quite impaired and learning to read can be very slow and problematic. Combinations of phonological problems are called a double deficit in the research. Students with double deficits are often the most impaired readers.

While each individual with naming problems is unique in terms of the severity of his or her retrieval problem as well as the nature of his or her other strengths and weaknesses, the following general principles and specific techniques are important for instruction:

- *Teach to the point of overlearning and automaticity.* Each critical reading skill that involves naming must be taught *beyond* the point of perfect performance until the skill is truly automatic. The process of initially learning a skill (such as the sounds associated with various letters and patterns) often takes much longer than expected, and the more severe the retrieval problem, the longer the period of time required to establish accuracy. After accuracy is achieved, the student must be given multiple opportunities to practice *accurate* recall of the information. For example, when the student is taught a new syllable pattern, they must be given practice reading words with that pattern. Practice should include work at the word level (for example, flash cards or word lists) as well as at the level of reading phrases, sentences, and passages containing the target patterns. Systematic and frequent *review* of information even after an item seems to be well established is critical. In addition to spending a portion of each lesson on review, some students require review and practice over weekends, holidays, and vacations to avoid the loss of skills.

- *Use decodable texts.* It is absolutely critical to use decodable reading materials (that is, material that contains multiple examples of the patterns being practiced). Decodable readers are quite different from leveled readers, which do not contain sufficient examples of the target patterns and encourage students to guess words based on the context or the first letter of the words. Guessing must be actively discouraged for students with naming problems as incorrect guesses (for example, looking at the word *the* and guessing *they* or *then*) actually make it more difficult for the student to learn the correct association.

- *Use cues to facilitate learning and recall.* To facilitate the initial learning of a skill involving naming, students should be given a set of cues. Effective cues include associating the information to be learned with a picture, key word, story, or gesture. For example, for each letter-sound association to be learned, provide the student with a picture and key word and practice until the association is automatic. Gestures can be used for students with more severe problems as well as for those associations that are difficult. Learning the "short" sounds of vowels is a good example of associations that can be successfully taught with gestures. Another type of cueing is to pair kinesthetic and tactile information with the information being learned. Examples include tracing a letter while making the sound that is being practiced as well as teaching a student to focus on how his or her mouth, lips, and tongue feel when certain sounds are produced. Provide adequate cues at each step of learning so the student does not practice making incorrect responses. Eventually, with sufficient practice, the information will be learned to the level of automaticity and cues will no longer be needed.

- *Reduce the number of "names" to be learned.* The most important way to accomplish this technique is to limit the number of *sight words* (words that must be memorized). Avoid the common practice of giving lists of high-frequency words for students to learn by *sight* (memorizing the "name" for an arbitrary string of letters). For students with naming problems, this practice is counter-productive and results in frustration and confusion. The alternative is to teach students to read using letter-sound associations and spelling patterns and reserve memorization for those few truly irregular words that cannot be decoded, for example, *have* or *said*. In the context of a research-based decoding program, focus instruction on the critical ingredients for reading and spelling by teaching to mastery a smaller than usual set of letter-sound associations (for example, one short vowel and a few selected consonants) in the context of a well-structured, code-based reading program. For younger students with more severe problems, it may be necessary to teach letter sounds alone, rather than the letter names, because learning both may be too difficult in the beginning of instruction.

Visual/Orthographic Processing Instruction and Support

Although the definition of dyslexia focuses on the importance of phonological processing skills, research and clinical observation make it clear that some students also have great difficulty developing the orthographic skills necessary for accurate and efficient reading and spelling. Orthographic memory is important for all types of words. For words with regular spelling patterns (that follow the rules of English), the ability to learn and quickly recognize the common patterns within words is critical for efficient reading and spelling. Words with irregular spelling patterns (that is, words that do not follow the rules of English) present an even greater challenge for students with poor orthographic processing skills. The automatic recognition of these words that include many high-frequency words, such as *come, want, does,* and *was,* are critical for reading. Another challenge is presented by words that sound the same but have different meanings based on their spellings. Examples include *read* and *reed, their* and *there,* and *birth* and *berth.* For words such as these and irregular words, good phonemic awareness skills and knowledge of letter-sound associations are not sufficient. The student must remember or recognize the specific string of letters that is appropriate for each word.

For students with dyslexia, the first step is to teach them the regular patterns of English (including letter-sound associations and spelling patterns) in a systematic way and then give them multiple encounters with these patterns within words until they are recognized automatically. Repeated practice reading words accurately using decoding and word analysis strategies leads to the ultimate development of orthographic memory for the patterns of English. The strategy of overlearning (described on page 64) is applicable in this context as many students with dyslexia require extensive amounts of practice for words to be recognized automatically.

For words with irregular or several variant spellings, additional strategies be required to develop what is referred to as *mental orthographic images.* A mental orthographic image (MOI) is a detailed and exact mental model of a word, a term that is often used interchangeably with sight words as described on page 66. Students who have difficulty developing orthographic images require direct instruction using strategies that include visualization and the use of multiple senses. Spelling and reading for irregular or variant spelling words should be taught together and specific strategies are described in the section on reading and spelling instruction below.

Reading

In addition to the memory and processing skills already described, assessments of dyslexia also include detailed information about specific reading and spelling skills. Recommendations for instruction in each of these areas are provided below:

- *Word identification.* Learning to read words accurately is the first step in becoming a competent reader. In addition to developing basic phonological awareness skills, students must master *phonics* or *word study*. *Phonics* refers to knowledge of the letters that are used to represent the sounds of English. The most effective way of teaching this information is to begin with the sounds of English and systematically teach students the connections to letters. First teach a sound and then anchor that information to the most common letter by using cues such as key words, pictures, and gestures. Gradually build up the student's knowledge of sounds and letters in English by moving from frequently used, simple letter-sound associations to more complex associations.

In addition to letter-sound associations, *word study* (also called *decoding, word attack,* or *word analysis*) should include instruction in the following areas:

- Syllables: six types of English syllables and patterns for division of words into syllables

- Morphology: base words, roots, prefixes, and suffixes

- Orthographic rules and patterns: words or parts of words that do not relate to the sounds must be taught explicitly so that students understand the reason for the spelling. An example is that no word in English can end in *v,* so words such as *love* must have an *e* on the end.

In each of these areas, the focus should be on teaching students to *recognize patterns within words* rather than rote memorization of rules. Effective instruction includes teachers and students actively analyzing the structure of words; sorting words into categories based on syllable pattern, morphology, or orthography; manipulating the sounds and letters of words to build new words; and the provision of a great deal of practice reading words containing the patterns being taught.

In English, there are also a few words that have truly irregular spellings that must be memorized. Because many of these words are frequently used in writing, it is important that students be taught to read such words correctly. Since these words cannot be read by the process of decoding, students must be taught these words in a different way. The first step is to teach the student to analyze words and identify the part or parts that do not follow the rules of English. For example, in the irregular word *said* it is the vowel team *ai* that does not follow the rules. After the irregular part is identified, students are taught using a structured procedure to memorize the correct pronunciation of the word.

- *Automaticity and reading fluency.* Reading with comprehension is an extremely complex task that involves more than reading accurately. All of the subskills of reading (sounds, letter names, pattern recognition, and word recognition) should be taught beyond accuracy until the skills become automatic. For many students with dyslexia, the transition from accurate but slow word reading to automatic and fast word recognition is very difficult. Such students require much more practice in accurately reading words before words are recognized automatically. Practice must be provided at the word and phrase level using materials that provide multiple examples of the patterns and words that are being practiced. At the word level, the student practices reading words grouped by patterns until the words can be read without being sounded out. Goals are set for the number of words read within a certain time frame and practice is carried out until the goals are met. The same process is used for phrases that contain high frequency, irregular words and words that can be sounded out (for example, *at the camp* or *in a shop*). The results are charted as a visual record of the progress the student is making.

    The ability to read words automatically is the most important factor in how fluently a student reads text. Other important factors are reading with expression and comprehension. Teaching students to read in phrases is one strategy that promotes fluent reading. The process of identifying phrases within sentences is modeled for students including scooping (that is, connecting words in a phrase with a curved line under the text) beneath each phrase as it is read. Then the student practices reading in this manner. The term *repeated reading* is used to describe various ways of encouraging students to read the same text three to four times. Short, frequent practice sessions using text at the student's instructional level or decodable passages is most effective. Students respond to concrete measures of progress, such as charting, and teachers should provide support, such as modeling, and work on word reading accuracy as needed for individual students. Fluency instruction should always be linked to comprehension of what has been read so the ultimate purpose of reading is clear to the student.

- *Comprehension and vocabulary.* A number of factors are important in determining a student's ability to comprehend text. In addition to skill in reading words accurately and automatically, knowledge of word meanings, background knowledge, awareness of the structure of text (at the sentence, paragraph, and text levels), as well as the ability to monitor what is being read and to use appropriate strategies are all important. The most effective instruction for improving comprehension involves teaching students a combination of strategies by first modeling and directly teaching the strategy and then providing guided practice in selecting and using each strategy appropriately. Strategies supported by sound research include comprehension monitoring, cooperative learning, graphic and semantic organizers, question answering and generation, story structure, and summarization.

Vocabulary development begins with the words that a child hears and continues as the child encounters words through reading. Reading widely in texts that contain mature vocabulary is a critical part of developing strong vocabulary knowledge and the ultimate goal for students with dyslexia. However, for students who do not read well and extensively, it is particularly important that vocabulary skills also be taught explicitly and thoroughly.

Effective methods of instruction include direct instruction using activities that actively engage the student as well as provide multiple exposures to targeted words with many opportunities to discuss and use the words. Another effective way to teach vocabulary is explicit instruction in the structure of words including roots, suffixes, and prefixes and how to use this information to determine the meaning of complex words. Using context to determine word meanings is an important skill that must be taught directly to many students, especially those who are struggling readers. Although using dictionaries alone is not an effective tool for developing vocabulary, students should be taught to use tools including technology for determining the meaning of words.

Spelling

Research has shown that there are strong connections between reading words and spelling words and between spelling skills and writing. In spite of these strong relationships, many educators consider spelling instruction as unnecessary even for students in elementary school. For students with dyslexia, spelling instruction is a critical part of teaching them to understand the structure of words in the English language and to use that knowledge to read and write competently. Simply learning to read does not ensure that students will become competent spellers. For all students, spelling instruction should be an integral part of literacy instruction beginning in kindergarten and continuing through middle school. It should progress from the simplest regular spelling patterns to more complex patterns including multisyllabic words, the six English syllable types, morphology, and then to Latin-based words and Greek combining forms. This same progression is important for students with dyslexia, and spelling must be carefully coordinated with reading instruction so that the student is taught the same skills for reading and for spelling.

Principles of instruction for poor spellers should include teacher-directed, systematic practice with controlled amounts of information: 5 to 6 new words per week with only 3 words per week for the most impaired readers. Instruction should include modeling with immediate, corrective feedback and should teach all elements of word structure in a systematic, sequential, and multisensory manner. Other strategies that are useful for words that follow the rules of English language include the use of guided discovery, analyzing and sorting words by patterns, and teaching spelling choices and basic rules concerning how to make changes to base words.

For words that do not follow the rules and have unexpected spellings that do not match the pronunciation, different instruction is necessary to help students develop accurate memory (Mental Orthographic Images or MOIs) for the letter strings specific to these words. Procedures useful for irregular words include analysis of the word to determine the irregular parts and the use of multisensory strategies (such as tracing the word in the air) and imagery (such as spelling the word with eyes closed and visualizing the written word). Spelling-based pronunciations (for example, *Wed-nes-day*) and mnemonics (for example, *the principal is your pal*) can also be useful for many students.

For all types of words that are taught, students should be given ample practice using words in writing (dictation and personal writing). Because spelling is more difficult than reading, progress is often slower, but all students can learn to be adequate spellers.

ACCOMMODATIONS AND MODIFICATIONS

In addition to instruction linked directly to assessment, many students with dyslexia also require accommodations, modifications, or both to be successful.

Accommodations for students with dyslexia involve changes in the way information (such as tasks or tests) is presented to students but do not alter the content of assignments or change what a test measures. The purpose of accommodations is to allow students with dyslexia to show what they know without being penalized for their disability. Accommodations allow a student to bypass the area of disability. Examples of accommodations for students with dyslexia, grouped by category include the following:

- Presentation (CD/audio tape, text-to-speech programs, large print, less information on a page, designated reader, instructions given orally)

- Response (verbal response, dictation to scribe, tape record responses, respond via computer, record in test booklet)
- Timing (breaks, extended time)
- Setting (preferential seating, special lighting or acoustics, small group setting, space with minimal distractions, private room)
- Test scheduling (several sessions over a day or several days, subtests taken in different order, tests administered at specific times of day)
- Other (special test preparation, provide on-task/focusing prompts, any reasonable accommodation needed that does not fit under above categories)

Technology is increasingly important for accommodations and many examples are relevant to components of reading. A few examples follow:

- Background knowledge and vocabulary (electronic references such as dictionaries, thesauruses, encyclopedias, video supports)
- Diagrams and animated illustrations
- Comprehension (digital text including Bookshare.org and Learning Ally) and text-to-speech (TTS)
- Software, annotations, and study skill features
- Reading and writing (spell checkers, word prediction software, graphic organizer software with outlining and drafting capabilities, voice recognition software)

In contrast, *modifications* refer to changes made to curriculum expectations to meet the specific needs of individual students with dyslexia. These changes can be minimal or complex and are provided when the student cannot meet the expectations because of his or her disability. Examples include modified reading and spelling assignments, modified grading, exemption from second language requirements, and provision of a modified language arts class with specialized remediation, or specially designed instruction as it is called in federal and state laws. For students with specific learning disabilities and dyslexia, information about the specially designed instruction as well as accommodations and modifications to the regular education program should be clearly described in the IEP.

The position paper in Table 2, from IDA and Learning Ally (formerly Recording for the Blind & Dyslexic), describes the treatment that is needed for students with dyslexia.

Table 2. Remediation and Accommodation in an Academic Setting – A Two-Pronged Approach

---

- Remediation and accommodation are distinct yet complementary interventions for individuals with dyslexia.

- Both are essential to school success for students with dyslexia.

- Remediation that is <u>evidence-based</u> and provides structured language instruction delivered in a direct and explicit manner in the major components of the reading process allows individuals with dyslexia to acquire skills associated with reading proficiency.

- Accommodations, such as recorded books and other assistive technologies, are among the ways individuals with dyslexia can access print and the content of the general education curricula more effectively.

- Individuals with dyslexia are entitled to both remediation and accommodation; one should not preclude the provision of the other. Together they allow the individual with dyslexia to participate and perform in accordance with his or her potential in the academic setting.

RFB&D/IDA 2005

In conclusion, students with diagnosed dyslexia need to receive more than the average amount of literacy instruction, delivered by a highly trained reading teacher who is knowledgeable about the structure of language. Early intervention and additional instruction in kindergarten through third grade are essential for struggling readers. Older students who are behind in reading and writing skills also need instruction to help them catch up to grade-level literacy skills. Students with dyslexia need to spend more time on task receiving direct instruction, and they need to practice correct responses in reading, spelling, and writing a sufficient number of times to achieve mastery or automaticity with literacy skills. Their curriculum, which should be highly structured, must integrate phonological processing, phonics, word study, and decoding together with fluency, vocabulary, and comprehension instruction. These students also need direct and systematic instruction in spelling and in writing. It bears repeating that the remedy for dyslexia, the most common specific learning disability or disorder, is instruction. U.S. federal law calls this "specially designed instruction," and a well-conducted evaluation illuminates the student's particular strengths and weaknesses. Assessment generates a student's unique learning profile, which is the first step in designing a learning plan that will help the struggling reader become a competent reader and writer.

AFTERWORD

The list of successful and even famous adults with dyslexia is extensive and informative. Students and adults with dyslexia can and do have fulfilling personal and professional lives. Adults with diagnosed dyslexia understand their unique learning profile and know when and if they need accommodations in the workplace. They know the symptoms of this common learning disorder and they intervene early to help family members who also experience struggles with literacy.

But none of that is possible without assessment. For students who struggle with literacy skill development, ongoing assessment is critical to provide accurate, reliable, and valid information about their present level of performance and academic skills. Detailed informed assessment, as outlined in these chapters, is crucial to determine if the student is experiencing a learning disorder such as dyslexia. Diagnosis of dyslexia is important to provide documentation for access to needed remediation and accommodation. Empowered with information from well-conducted assessment, students, parents, and teachers understand the specific learning needs of the student, know what is needed for mastery of skills at each age and grade level, and have the expertise needed to provide the necessary amount of well-designed instruction, accommodations, and modifications to help each student achieve his or her potential in school and beyond.

Students and adults with diagnosed dyslexia often become strong self-advocates, able to describe their learning needs and obtain the accommodations they need in educational and career settings. They have learned that hard work and perseverance is part of life and failure only means that you must try harder to master challenging skills. Many with dyslexia say that understanding their own unique learning profile gives them greater empathy for the strengths and weaknesses of others—an important insight for us all.

References

Chapter 1: Becoming a Reader

Adams, M. J., Foorman, B. R., Lundberg, I., & Bleeler, T. (1998). *Phonemic awareness in young children: A classroom curriculum.* Baltimore, MD: Paul H. Brookes.

Chall, J. S. (1983). *Stages of reading development.* New York, NY: McGraw Hill.

Fowler, C. A. (2011). How theories of phonology may enhance understanding of the role of phonology in reading development and reading disability. In S. A. Brady, D. Braze, & C. A. Fowler (Eds.), *Explaining individual differences in reading: Theory and evidence* (pp. 3–19). New York, NY: Taylor and Francis.

Gough, P., & Tunmer, W. (1986). The simple view of reading. *Reading and Writing, An Interdisciplinary Journal, 2,* 127–160.

Henry, M. (2010). *Unlocking literacy: Effective decoding and spelling instruction, 2nd edition.* Baltimore, MD: Paul H. Brookes.

Liberman, I. Y., & Shankweiler, D. (1991). Phonology and beginning reading: A tutorial. In L. Rieben & C. A. Perfetti (Eds.), *Learning to read: Basic research and its implications* (pp. 3–17). Hillsdale, NJ: Lawrence Erlbaum Associates.

Lowell, S. C. (2011, Summer). Best practices in reading instruction: An international effort. *Perspectives on Language and Literacy, 37*(3), 41.

Moats, L. C. (2005). *LETRS: Language essentials for teachers of reading and spelling.* Longmont, CO: Sopris West.

Moats, L. C., & Dakin, K. E. (2008). *Basic facts about dyslexia and other reading problems.* Baltimore, MD: The International Dyslexia Association.

National Institutes of Child Health and Human Development (NICHD). (2000). *Report of the National Reading Panel. Teaching children to read: An evidence-based assessment of the scientific literature on reading and its implications for reading instruction.* Bethesda, MD: NICHD, NIH. Retrieved from http://www.nationalreadingpanel.org/default.htm

National Institute for Literacy and National Institute for Family Literacy. (2009). *Developing early literacy: Report of the National Early Literacy Panel.* Retrieved from http://lincs.ed.gov/earlychildhood/NELP/NELPreport.html

RAND Reading Study Group. (2002). *Reading for understanding: Toward an R&D program in reading comprehension.* Santa Monica, CA: RAND Corporation.

Robinson, A. (1995). *The story of writing.* New York, NY: Thames and Hudson, Ltd.

Chapter 2: The Prevalence of Reading Problems and Dyslexia

Adams, M. J. (1998). *Beginning to read: Thinking and learning about print.* Cambridge, MA: MIT Press.

American Psychiatric Association (APA). (2013). *Diagnostic and statistical manual of mental disorders-5.* Washington, DC: Author.

Cunningham, A. E., & Stanovich, K. E. (1999). What reading does for the mind. *American Educator, 22*(1–2), 8–15.

Fletcher, J., Lyon, R., Fuchs, L., & Barnes, M. (2007). *Learning disabilities, from identification to intervention.* New York, NY: The Guilford Press.

Henry, M. (2010). *Unlocking literacy: Effective decoding and spelling instruction, 2nd edition*. Baltimore, MD: Paul H. Brookes.

Hook, P., & Haynes, C. (2009). Reading and writing in child language disorders. In R. Schwartz (Ed.), *Handbook of child language disorders*. New York, NY: Psychology Press.

Individuals with Disabilities Education Improvement Act of 2004, PL 108-446, 20 U.S.C. §§ 1400 *et seq.*

(The) International Dyslexia Association. (2008). *Definition of dyslexia*. Retrieved from http://www.interdys.org/FactSheets.htm

(The) International Dyslexia Association. (2012). *Dyslexia basics*. Retrieved from http://www.interdys.org/FactSheets.htm

(The) International Dyslexia Association & Recording for the Blind and Dyslexic (RFB&D). (2005). *Five principles of remediation and accommodation in an academic setting* [Joint Statement]. Available from http://www.interdys.org/Advocacy.htm

Moats, L. C., & Dakin, K. E. (2008). *Basic facts about dyslexia and other reading problems*. Baltimore, MD: The International Dyslexia Association.

National Center for Education Statistics (NCES). (2011). *Nation's report card: National assessment of educational progress*. Washington, DC: U.S. Department of Education.

Orton, S. T. (1989). (original 1937, W. Norton & Co., Inc.; renewed 1964). *Reading, writing, and speech problems in children and selected papers*. Austin, TX: PRO-ED and The Orton Dyslexia Society.

Pennington, B. (2009). *Diagnosing learning disorders, second edition*. New York, NY: The Guilford Press.

Torgesen, J. K. (2004). Lessons learned from research on interventions for students who have difficulty learning to read. In P. McCardle & V. Chhabra (Eds.), *The voice of evidence in reading research* (pp. 355–382). Baltimore, MD: Paul H. Brookes.

World Health Organization. *ICD-10: International statistical classification of diseases and related health problems–10th revision.* Endorsed by the Forty-third World Health Assembly in May, 1990. Available from www.who.int/classifications/icd/ICD-10_2nd_ed_volume2.pdf

Chapter 3: Types of Assessment: Screening, Progress Monitoring, Outcomes, and Diagnostic

Adams, M. (1990). *Beginning to read: Thinking and learning about print.* Cambridge, MA: MIT Press.

Badian, N. (2005). Does a visual-orthographic deficit contribute to reading disability? *Annals of Dyslexia, 55,* 28–52.

Bashir, A., & Hook, P. (2009). Fluency: A key link between word identification and comprehension. *Language, Speech and Hearing Services in the Schools, 40,* 196–200.

Berninger, V., Stage, S., Smith, D., & Hildebrand, D. (2001). Assessment for reading and writing intervention: A 3-tier model for prevention and intervention. In J. Andrews, D. Saklofske, & H. Janzen (Eds.), *Ability, achievement, and behavior assessment: A practical handbook* (pp. 195–223). New York, NY: Academic Press.

Carlisle, J. (2003). Morphology matters in learning to read: A commentary. *Reading Psychology, 24,* 291–322.

Ehri, L. (1998). Grapheme–phoneme knowledge is essential for learning to read words in English. In J. Metsala & L. Ehri (Eds.), *Word recognition in beginning reading* (pp. 3–40). Hillsdale, NJ: Erlbaum.

Fletcher, J. M. (2006, Winter). The need for response to intervention models of learning disabilities. *Perspectives on Language and Literacy, 32*(1), 12–15.

Fuchs, D., & Fuchs, L. (2006). Introduction to Response to Intervention: What, why, and how valid is it? *Reading Research Quarterly, 41,* 93–99.

Fuchs, L. S., Fuchs, D., Hosp, M. D., & Jenkins, J. (2001). Oral reading fluency as an indicator of reading competence: A theoretical, empirical, and historical analysis. *Scientific Studies of Reading, 5,* 239–259.

Good, R., & Kaminski, R. (Eds.). (2010). *Dynamic Indicators of Basic Early Literacy Skills Next (DIBELS Next).* Eugene, OR: Institute for the Development of Educational Achievement.

Hook, P., & Haynes, C. (2009). Reading and writing in child language disorders. In R. Schwartz (Ed.), *Handbook of child language disorders.* New York, NY: Psychology Press.

Kamhi, A., & Catts, H. (2012). *Language and reading disabilities (3rd ed.).* Boston, MA: Pearson.

Kuhn, M., Meisinger, E., & Schwanenflugel, P. (2010). Aligning theory and assessment of reading fluency: Automaticity, prosody, and definitions of fluency. *Reading Research Quarterly, 45,* 230.

MacGinitie, W., MacGinitie, R., Maria, K., Dreyer, L., & Hughes, K. (2002). *Gates-MacGinitie Reading Tests® (GMRT®) Fourth Edition.* Rolling Meadows, IL: Riverside.

Mather, N., Hammill, D., Allen, E., & Roberts, R. (2004). *TOS-WRF: Test of silent word reading fluency: Examiner's manual.* Austin, TX: PRO-ED.

Meyer, M., & Felton, R. (1999). Repeated reading to enhance fluency: Old approaches and new directions. *Annals of Dyslexia, 49,* 283–306.

National Early Literacy Panel. (2008). *Developing early literacy: Report of the National Early Literacy Panel. Executive summary.* Washington, DC: National Institute for Literacy.

National Reading Panel. (2000). *Teaching children to read: An evidence-based assessment of the scientific research literature on reading and its implications for reading instruction.* (NIH Publication No. 00–4754). Washington, DC: U.S. Government Printing Office. Available at http://www.nationalreadingpanel.org/

Pearson Publishing. (2012). *Stanford Achievement Test Series, Tenth Edition*. San Antonio, TX: Author.

Rashotte, C. A., & Torgesen, J. K. (1985). Repeated reading and reading fluency in learning disabled children. *Reading Research Quarterly, 20*, 180–188.

Rasinski, T. (1990). Effects of repeated reading and listening-while-reading on reading fluency. *Journal of Educational Research, 83(3)*, 147–150.

Robertson, C., & Salter, W. (2007). *The Phonological Awareness Test 2 (PAT 2)*. East Moline, IL: LinguiSystems.

Snow, C. E., Burns, M. S., & Griffin, P. (Eds.). (1998). *Preventing reading difficulties in young children*. Washington, DC: National Academy Press.

Spear-Swerling, L. (2006). Children's reading comprehension and oral reading fluency in easy text. *Reading and Writing, 19*, 199–220.

Stackhouse, J., & Wells, B. (1997). How do speech and language problems affect literacy development? In C. Hulme & M. Snowling (Eds.), *Dyslexia: Biology, cognition, and intervention* (pp. 182–211). London: Whurr.

Torgesen, J. K. (2006). *A comprehensive K–3 reading assessment plan: Guidance for school leaders*. Portsmouth, NH: RMC Research Corporation, Center on Instruction.

Vellutino, F. R., Scanlon, D. M., Small, S., & Fanuele, D. P. (2006). Response to intervention as a vehicle for distinguishing between children with and without reading disabilities: Evidence for the role of kindergarten and first-grade interventions. *Journal of Learning Disabilities, 38*, 157–169.

Wagner, R., Torgesen, J., & Rashotte, C. (1999). *Comprehensive Test of Phonological Processing (CTOPP)*. Austin, TX: PRO-ED.

Wiederholt, J., & Bryant, B. (2012). *Gray Oral Reading Tests–Fifth Edition (GORT-5)*. Austin, TX: PRO-ED.

Williams, K. (2001). *Group Reading Assessment and Diagnostic Evaluation (GRADE)*, level 3. Circle Pines, MN: American Guidance Services.

Woodcock, R. (2011). *Woodcock Reading Mastery Tests, Third Edition (WRMT™-III)*. San Antonio, TX: Pearson.

Chapter 4: Clinical Evaluation of Dyslexia

Aaron, P. G., Joshi, R. M., & Quatroche, D. (2008). *Becoming a professional reading teacher*. Baltimore, MD: Paul H. Brookes.

Fletcher, J., Lyon, R., Fuchs, L., & Barnes, M. (2007). *Learning disabilities, from identification to intervention*. New York, NY: The Guilford Press.

(The) International Dyslexia Association. (2008). *Definition of dyslexia*. Retrieved from http://www.interdys.org/FactSheets.htm

(The) International Dyslexia Association. (2012). *Dyslexia basics*. Retrieved from http://www.interdys.org/FactSheets.htm

Mazzocco, M. M. M. (Ed.). (2011). Mathematical difficulties in school age children. *Perspectives on Language and Literacy, 37*(2).

Rathvon, N. (2004). *Early reading assessment: A practitioner's handbook*. New York, NY: The Guilford Press.

Chapter 5: Linking Assessment to Instruction: Recommendations for Educational Programming

Berninger, V. W., & Wolf, B. J. (2009). *Teaching students with dyslexia and dysgraphia*. Baltimore, MD: Paul H. Brookes.

Birsh, J. R. (Ed.). (2011). *Multisensory teaching of basic language skills (3rd ed.)*. Baltimore, MD: Paul H. Brookes.

Carreker, S. (2011). Teaching reading: Accurate decoding. In J. R. Birsh (Ed.), *Multisensory teaching of basic language skills (3rd ed.)*. Baltimore, MD: Paul H. Brookes.

Farrall, M. L. (2012). *Reading assessment linking language, literacy, and cognition.* Hoboken, NJ: John Wiley & Sons.

Felton, R. H. (2001). Students with three types of severe reading disabilities: Introduction to the case studies. *Journal of Special Education, 35*(3), 122–124.

Fielding, L., Kerr, N., & Rosier, P. (2007). *Annual growth for all students, catch-up growth for those who are behind.* Kennewick, WA: The New Foundation Press.

McCardle, P., & Chhabra, V. (Eds.). (2004). *The voice of evidence in reading research.* Baltimore, MD: Paul H. Brookes.

McEwan, E. K. (2009). *Teach them all to read (2nd ed.).* Thousand Oaks, CA: Corwin.

McKenna, M. C., & Dougherty Stahl, K. A. (2009). *Assessment for reading instruction (2nd ed.).* New York, NY: The Guilford Press.

Moats, L. C., Dakin, K. E., & Joshi, R. M. (Eds.). (2012). *Expert perspectives on interventions for reading.* Baltimore, MD: The International Dyslexia Association.

National Center for Learning Disabilities (NCLD). (2006). *Accommodations for students with LD.* Available from http://www.ldonline.org/article/Accommodations_for_Students_with_LD?theme=print

National Center for Technology Innovation and Center for Implementing Technology in Education (CITEd). (2010). *Adolescent literacy: What's technology got to do with it?* Washington, DC: AdLit.org.

Rathvon, N. (2004). *Early reading assessment.* New York, NY: The Guilford Press.

Wolf, M., & Bowers, P. G. (2000). Naming-speed processes and developmental reading disabilities: An introduction to the special issue on the double-deficit hypothesis. *Journal of Learning Disabilities, 33*(4), 322–324.

Printed in the USA
CPSIA information can be obtained
at www.ICGtesting.com
LVHW021907060124
768317LV00004B/175